87 Breakfast Recipes for Home

By: Kelly Johnson

Table of Contents

Recipes
- Classic Pancakes
- Blueberry Pancakes
- Banana Pancakes
- Chocolate Chip Pancakes
- French Toast
- Cinnamon French Toast
- Waffles
- Oatmeal with Berries
- Overnight Oats
- Greek Yogurt Parfait
- Fruit Salad
- Avocado Toast
- Smashed Avocado and Egg Toast
- Veggie Omelette
- Spinach and Feta Omelette
- Western Omelette
- Quiche Lorraine
- Breakfast Burrito
- Breakfast Quesadilla
- Breakfast Tacos
- Huevos Rancheros
- Shakshuka
- Eggs Benedict

- Eggs Florentine
- Breakfast Pizza
- Breakfast Sandwich
- Bagel with Cream Cheese and Lox
- Smoked Salmon and Avocado Bagel
- Granola with Yogurt
- Smoothie Bowl
- Acai Bowl
- Chia Seed Pudding
- Breakfast Casserole
- Hash Browns
- Sweet Potato Hash
- Bacon and Egg Muffins
- Sausage and Cheese Biscuits
- Cinnamon Rolls
- Breakfast Sliders
- Spinach and Cheese Strata
- Baked Eggs in Tomato Sauce
- Breakfast Stir-Fry
- Breakfast Skewers
- Pumpkin Pancakes
- Apple Cinnamon Oatmeal
- Peanut Butter Banana Toast
- Breakfast Stuffed Peppers
- Greek Frittata
- Raspberry Almond Scones
- Banana Nut Muffins

- Zucchini Bread
- Caramelized Onion and Bacon Quiche
- Breakfast BLT
- Cranberry Orange Muffins
- Nutella Stuffed French Toast
- Spinach and Mushroom Breakfast Wrap
- Chocolate Peanut Butter Smoothie
- Breakfast Nachos
- Breakfast Pizza Rolls
- Breakfast Sushi
- Pumpkin Spice Pancakes
- Maple Pecan Granola
- Biscuits and Gravy
- Dutch Baby Pancake
- Breakfast Fajitas
- Ham and Cheese Croissant
- Breakfast Polenta with Poached Egg
- Lemon Poppy Seed Pancakes
- Blueberry Banana Bread
- Breakfast Bruschetta
- Cheesy Grits
- Breakfast Empanadas
- Caprese Avocado Toast
- Mango Coconut Chia Pudding
- Breakfast Tostadas
- Breakfast Slaw
- Bacon and Spinach Breakfast Wrap

- Oat Bran Muffins
- Pesto and Tomato Breakfast Sandwich
- Sausage Gravy Biscuits
- Ricotta Pancakes
- Blackberry Lemon Scones
- Breakfast Pita Pockets
- Breakfast Stuffed Mushrooms
- Sweet Potato Pancakes
- Breakfast Flatbread
- Breakfast Enchiladas

Classic Pancakes

Ingredients:

- 1 cup all-purpose flour
- 2 tablespoons sugar
- 1 teaspoon baking powder
- 1/2 teaspoon baking soda
- 1/4 teaspoon salt
- 3/4 cup buttermilk
- 1/4 cup milk
- 1 large egg
- 2 tablespoons unsalted butter, melted
- Cooking spray or additional butter for greasing the pan

Instructions:

In a large mixing bowl, whisk together the flour, sugar, baking powder, baking soda, and salt.
In a separate bowl, whisk together the buttermilk, milk, egg, and melted butter.
Pour the wet ingredients into the dry ingredients and stir until just combined. It's okay if there are a few lumps.
Heat a griddle or non-stick skillet over medium heat. Lightly coat with cooking spray or butter.
Pour 1/4 cup of batter onto the griddle for each pancake. Cook until bubbles form on the surface, then flip and cook until the other side is golden brown.
Repeat until all the batter is used.

Serve the pancakes warm with your favorite toppings such as maple syrup, fresh fruit, or whipped cream.

Enjoy your classic pancakes!

Blueberry Pancakes

Ingredients:

- 1 cup all-purpose flour
- 2 tablespoons sugar
- 1 teaspoon baking powder
- 1/2 teaspoon baking soda
- 1/4 teaspoon salt
- 3/4 cup buttermilk
- 1/4 cup milk
- 1 large egg
- 2 tablespoons unsalted butter, melted
- 1 cup fresh or frozen blueberries
- Cooking spray or additional butter for greasing the pan

Instructions:

In a large mixing bowl, whisk together the flour, sugar, baking powder, baking soda, and salt.

In a separate bowl, whisk together the buttermilk, milk, egg, and melted butter.

Pour the wet ingredients into the dry ingredients and stir until just combined. Gently fold in the blueberries.

Heat a griddle or non-stick skillet over medium heat. Lightly coat with cooking spray or butter.

Pour 1/4 cup of batter onto the griddle for each pancake. Cook until bubbles form on the surface, then flip and cook until the other side is golden brown.

Repeat until all the batter is used.

Serve the blueberry pancakes warm with additional blueberries on top and your favorite syrup.

Enjoy these delicious blueberry pancakes!

Banana Pancakes

Ingredients:

- 1 cup all-purpose flour
- 1 tablespoon sugar
- 1 teaspoon baking powder
- 1/2 teaspoon baking soda
- 1/4 teaspoon salt
- 1 large ripe banana, mashed
- 3/4 cup buttermilk
- 1/4 cup milk
- 1 large egg
- 2 tablespoons unsalted butter, melted
- Cooking spray or additional butter for greasing the pan

Instructions:

In a large mixing bowl, whisk together the flour, sugar, baking powder, baking soda, and salt.

In a separate bowl, mash the ripe banana and then whisk in the buttermilk, milk, egg, and melted butter.

Pour the wet ingredients into the dry ingredients and stir until just combined.

Heat a griddle or non-stick skillet over medium heat. Lightly coat with cooking spray or butter.

Pour 1/4 cup of batter onto the griddle for each pancake. Cook until bubbles form on the surface, then flip and cook until the other side is golden brown.

Repeat until all the batter is used.

Serve the banana pancakes warm with sliced bananas on top and your favorite syrup.

Enjoy these delicious banana pancakes!

Chocolate Chip Pancakes

Ingredients:

- 1 cup all-purpose flour
- 2 tablespoons sugar
- 1 teaspoon baking powder
- 1/2 teaspoon baking soda
- 1/4 teaspoon salt
- 3/4 cup buttermilk
- 1/4 cup milk
- 1 large egg
- 2 tablespoons unsalted butter, melted
- 1/2 cup chocolate chips
- Cooking spray or additional butter for greasing the pan

Instructions:

In a large mixing bowl, whisk together the flour, sugar, baking powder, baking soda, and salt.

In a separate bowl, whisk together the buttermilk, milk, egg, and melted butter.

Pour the wet ingredients into the dry ingredients and stir until just combined. Gently fold in the chocolate chips.

Heat a griddle or non-stick skillet over medium heat. Lightly coat with cooking spray or butter.

Pour 1/4 cup of batter onto the griddle for each pancake. Sprinkle additional chocolate chips on the surface if desired. Cook until bubbles form on the surface, then flip and cook until the other side is golden brown.

Repeat until all the batter is used.

Serve the chocolate chip pancakes warm with additional chocolate chips on top and your favorite syrup.

Enjoy these delicious chocolate chip pancakes!

French Toast

Ingredients:

- 4 slices of bread (white or whole wheat)
- 2 large eggs
- 1/2 cup milk
- 1 teaspoon vanilla extract
- 1/2 teaspoon ground cinnamon
- Pinch of salt
- Butter or cooking spray for greasing the pan
- Optional toppings: maple syrup, powdered sugar, fresh fruit, whipped cream

Instructions:

In a shallow bowl, whisk together the eggs, milk, vanilla extract, ground cinnamon, and a pinch of salt.

Heat a griddle or non-stick skillet over medium heat. Add a little butter or use cooking spray to coat the surface.

Dip each slice of bread into the egg mixture, ensuring both sides are well-coated.

Place the coated bread slices on the heated griddle or skillet.

Cook each side until golden brown, usually 2-3 minutes per side.

Once cooked, transfer the French toasts to a plate.

Serve warm with your favorite toppings such as maple syrup, powdered sugar, fresh fruit, or whipped cream.

Enjoy your delicious homemade French Toast!

Cinnamon French Toast

Ingredients:

- 4 slices of bread (white or whole wheat)
- 2 large eggs
- 1/2 cup milk
- 1 teaspoon vanilla extract
- 1 teaspoon ground cinnamon
- Pinch of salt
- Butter or cooking spray for greasing the pan
- Optional toppings: maple syrup, powdered sugar, sliced bananas, chopped nuts

Instructions:

In a shallow bowl, whisk together the eggs, milk, vanilla extract, ground cinnamon, and a pinch of salt.

Heat a griddle or non-stick skillet over medium heat. Add a little butter or use cooking spray to coat the surface.

Dip each slice of bread into the egg mixture, ensuring both sides are well-coated.

Place the coated bread slices on the heated griddle or skillet.

Cook each side until golden brown, usually 2-3 minutes per side.

Once cooked, transfer the Cinnamon French toasts to a plate.

Serve warm with your favorite toppings such as maple syrup, powdered sugar, sliced bananas, or chopped nuts.

Enjoy the delightful flavor of Cinnamon French Toast!

Waffles

Ingredients:

- 2 cups all-purpose flour
- 2 tablespoons sugar
- 1 tablespoon baking powder
- 1/2 teaspoon salt
- 1 3/4 cups milk
- 1/3 cup vegetable oil
- 2 large eggs
- 1 teaspoon vanilla extract
- Cooking spray or additional oil for greasing the waffle iron

Instructions:

Preheat your waffle iron according to the manufacturer's instructions.

In a large mixing bowl, whisk together the flour, sugar, baking powder, and salt.

In a separate bowl, whisk together the milk, vegetable oil, eggs, and vanilla extract.

Pour the wet ingredients into the dry ingredients and stir until just combined. It's okay if there are a few lumps.

Lightly coat the waffle iron with cooking spray or oil.

Pour the batter onto the center of the preheated waffle iron, spreading it slightly towards the edges.

Close the waffle iron and cook according to the manufacturer's instructions, usually for about 5 minutes or until the waffles are golden brown and crisp.

Carefully remove the waffles and repeat with the remaining batter.

Serve the waffles warm with your favorite toppings such as maple syrup, whipped cream, fresh fruit, or chocolate chips.

Enjoy your delicious homemade waffles!

Oatmeal with Berries

Ingredients:

- 1 cup old-fashioned oats
- 2 cups milk (dairy or plant-based)
- 1/2 teaspoon vanilla extract
- 1/4 teaspoon ground cinnamon
- Pinch of salt
- Fresh berries (strawberries, blueberries, raspberries, etc.)
- Honey or maple syrup for sweetness (optional)
- Chopped nuts or seeds for garnish (optional)

Instructions:

In a saucepan, combine the oats, milk, vanilla extract, ground cinnamon, and a pinch of salt.
Bring the mixture to a gentle boil over medium heat, stirring occasionally.
Once it reaches a boil, reduce the heat to low and simmer for about 5 minutes or until the oats are cooked and the mixture thickens.
Remove the saucepan from heat and let it sit for a minute to thicken further.
Spoon the oatmeal into bowls.
Top the oatmeal with fresh berries. You can use a mix of berries for a variety of flavors.
Drizzle honey or maple syrup over the top for sweetness, if desired.
Garnish with chopped nuts or seeds for added texture and nutrition.
Serve the oatmeal with berries warm and enjoy a nutritious and delicious breakfast!

Feel free to customize the recipe with your favorite berries and toppings.
Overnight Oats

Ingredients:

- 1/2 cup old-fashioned oats
- 1/2 cup milk (dairy or plant-based)
- 1/4 cup yogurt (Greek yogurt works well)
- 1-2 tablespoons chia seeds (optional)
- 1/2 teaspoon vanilla extract
- 1-2 tablespoons sweetener (maple syrup, honey, or agave syrup)
- Fresh fruits, nuts, or seeds for toppings

Instructions:

In a jar or container with a lid, combine the oats, milk, yogurt, chia seeds (if using), vanilla extract, and sweetener.

Stir the ingredients until well combined.

Seal the jar or container with a lid and refrigerate overnight or for at least 4 hours. This allows the oats to soak and soften.

In the morning, give the overnight oats a good stir. If the mixture is too thick, you can add a bit more milk to reach your desired consistency.

Top the overnight oats with fresh fruits, nuts, or seeds of your choice.

Enjoy your delicious and convenient overnight oats!

Feel free to customize this recipe with your favorite toppings and sweeteners. It's a versatile and easy-to-make breakfast option.

Greek Yogurt Parfait

Ingredients:

- 1 cup Greek yogurt (plain or flavored)
- 1/2 cup granola
- 1/2 cup mixed berries (strawberries, blueberries, raspberries)
- 1 tablespoon honey or maple syrup (optional)
- 1/4 cup chopped nuts (almonds, walnuts, or your choice)
- Fresh mint leaves for garnish (optional)

Instructions:

In a glass or a bowl, start by layering about 1/4 cup of Greek yogurt at the bottom.

Add a layer of granola on top of the yogurt.

Next, add a layer of mixed berries.

Repeat the layers until you reach the top of the glass or bowl.

If desired, drizzle honey or maple syrup over the top for added sweetness.

Sprinkle chopped nuts on the top layer for extra crunch and nutrition.

Garnish with fresh mint leaves for a burst of freshness (optional).

Repeat the process for additional parfaits if making more than one.

Serve immediately and enjoy your delicious and nutritious Greek Yogurt Parfait!

Feel free to customize the parfait by adding your favorite fruits, nuts, or seeds. It's a versatile recipe that you can tailor to your taste preferences.

Fruit Salad

Ingredients:

- 2 cups fresh strawberries, hulled and halved
- 1 cup fresh blueberries
- 1 cup fresh grapes, halved
- 1 cup pineapple chunks
- 1 cup watermelon cubes
- 1 cup kiwi slices
- 1 banana, sliced
- Optional: Mint leaves for garnish

For the Honey-Lime Dressing:

- 2 tablespoons honey
- 1 tablespoon fresh lime juice
- Zest of one lime

Instructions:

In a large mixing bowl, combine all the prepared fruits.

In a separate small bowl, whisk together the honey, fresh lime juice, and lime zest to create the dressing.

Pour the honey-lime dressing over the fruits and gently toss until all the fruits are evenly coated.

Optional: Garnish with fresh mint leaves for added flavor.

Chill the fruit salad in the refrigerator for at least 30 minutes before serving.

Serve the fruit salad chilled as a refreshing side dish or dessert.

Feel free to customize the fruit selection based on your preferences or what's in season. This fruit salad is not only delicious but also a colorful and healthy option. Enjoy!

Avocado Toast

Ingredients:

- 1 ripe avocado
- 2 slices of your favorite bread (whole grain, sourdough, etc.)
- Salt and pepper to taste
- Optional toppings: cherry tomatoes, radish slices, poached egg, feta cheese, chili flakes, or herbs like cilantro or parsley

Instructions:

Toast the bread slices to your desired level of crispiness.

While the bread is toasting, cut the ripe avocado in half, remove the pit, and scoop the flesh into a bowl.

Mash the avocado with a fork until it reaches your desired consistency. You can leave it a bit chunky or make it smoother.

Season the mashed avocado with salt and pepper to taste.

Once the bread is toasted, spread the mashed avocado evenly over each slice.

Add your favorite toppings. Common choices include sliced cherry tomatoes, radish slices, a poached egg, feta cheese, chili flakes, or herbs.

Serve immediately and enjoy your delicious Avocado Toast!

This is a basic recipe, and you can get creative with toppings based on your preferences. Avocado Toast is not only tasty but also a nutritious option for breakfast or a quick snack.

Smashed Avocado and Egg Toast

Ingredients:

- 1 ripe avocado
- 2 slices of your favorite bread (whole grain, sourdough, etc.)
- Salt and pepper to taste
- 2 eggs
- Optional toppings: cherry tomatoes, arugula, feta cheese, chili flakes, or herbs like chives or parsley

Instructions:

Toast the bread slices to your desired level of crispiness.

While the bread is toasting, cut the ripe avocado in half, remove the pit, and scoop the flesh into a bowl.

Mash the avocado with a fork until it reaches your desired consistency. Season with salt and pepper to taste.

In a separate pan, cook the eggs to your liking. You can fry, poach, or scramble them.

Once the bread is toasted, spread the mashed avocado evenly over each slice.

Place the cooked eggs on top of the mashed avocado.

Add your favorite toppings. Consider sliced cherry tomatoes, arugula, crumbled feta cheese, chili flakes, or herbs like chives or parsley.

Season with additional salt and pepper if desired.

Serve immediately and enjoy your delicious Smashed Avocado and Egg Toast!

This combination makes for a hearty and satisfying breakfast or brunch option. Feel free to customize it with your favorite ingredients.

Veggie Omelette

Ingredients:

- 3 large eggs

- Salt and pepper to taste
- 1 tablespoon butter or cooking oil
- 1/4 cup diced bell peppers (any color)
- 1/4 cup diced onions
- 1/4 cup diced tomatoes
- 1/4 cup sliced mushrooms
- 1/4 cup chopped spinach or kale
- Optional: Grated cheese (cheddar, feta, or your choice)

Instructions:

Crack the eggs into a bowl and beat them with a fork or whisk. Season with salt and pepper to taste.

Heat butter or cooking oil in a non-stick skillet over medium heat.

Add diced bell peppers, onions, tomatoes, mushrooms, and chopped spinach or kale to the skillet. Sauté the vegetables until they are tender but still slightly crisp.

Push the sautéed vegetables to one side of the skillet.

Pour the beaten eggs into the empty side of the skillet.

Allow the eggs to set for a moment, then gently stir the eggs and vegetables together.

Continue cooking, lifting the edges to let the uncooked eggs flow underneath, until the eggs are mostly set.

If desired, sprinkle grated cheese over one half of the omelette.

Carefully fold the omelette in half with a spatula.

Cook for an additional minute or until the cheese is melted, and the omelette is cooked to your liking.

Slide the Veggie Omelette onto a plate and serve hot.

Feel free to customize the vegetables and cheese to suit your preferences. Enjoy your delicious and nutritious Veggie Omelette!

Spinach and Feta Omelette

Ingredients:

- 3 large eggs
- Salt and pepper to taste
- 1 tablespoon butter or cooking oil
- 1 cup fresh spinach, chopped
- 1/4 cup crumbled feta cheese
- Optional: Diced tomatoes, sliced mushrooms, or chopped onions

Instructions:

Crack the eggs into a bowl and beat them with a fork or whisk. Season with salt and pepper to taste.

Heat butter or cooking oil in a non-stick skillet over medium heat.

Add fresh spinach to the skillet and sauté until it wilts, usually for about 1-2 minutes.

If desired, add diced tomatoes, sliced mushrooms, or chopped onions to the skillet and sauté until they are tender.

Push the sautéed vegetables to one side of the skillet.

Pour the beaten eggs into the empty side of the skillet.

Allow the eggs to set for a moment, then gently stir the eggs and vegetables together.

Sprinkle crumbled feta cheese evenly over one half of the omelette.

Continue cooking, lifting the edges to let the uncooked eggs flow underneath, until the eggs are mostly set.

Carefully fold the omelette in half with a spatula.

Cook for an additional minute or until the cheese is melted, and the omelette is cooked to your liking.

Slide the Spinach and Feta Omelette onto a plate and serve hot.

Enjoy this flavorful and nutritious Spinach and Feta Omelette!

Western Omelette

Ingredients:

- 3 large eggs
- Salt and pepper to taste
- 1 tablespoon butter or cooking oil
- 1/4 cup diced ham
- 1/4 cup diced bell peppers (any color)
- 1/4 cup diced onions
- 1/4 cup shredded cheddar cheese
- Optional: Sliced mushrooms or diced tomatoes

Instructions:

Crack the eggs into a bowl and beat them with a fork or whisk. Season with salt and pepper to taste.

Heat butter or cooking oil in a non-stick skillet over medium heat.

Add diced ham, diced bell peppers, and diced onions to the skillet. Sauté until the vegetables are tender.

If desired, add sliced mushrooms or diced tomatoes to the skillet and sauté until they are tender.

Push the sautéed vegetables and ham to one side of the skillet.

Pour the beaten eggs into the empty side of the skillet.

Allow the eggs to set for a moment, then gently stir the eggs and vegetables together.

Sprinkle shredded cheddar cheese evenly over one half of the omelette.

Continue cooking, lifting the edges to let the uncooked eggs flow underneath, until the eggs are mostly set.

Carefully fold the omelette in half with a spatula.

Cook for an additional minute or until the cheese is melted, and the omelette is cooked to your liking.

Slide the Western Omelette onto a plate and serve hot.

Enjoy this classic Western Omelette with a hearty combination of ham, peppers, onions, and cheese!

Quiche Lorraine

Ingredients:

For the Pie Crust:

- 1 1/4 cups all-purpose flour
- 1/2 cup unsalted butter, cold and diced
- 1/4 teaspoon salt
- 3-4 tablespoons ice water

For the Filling:

- 8 slices bacon, cooked and crumbled
- 1 cup shredded Gruyère or Swiss cheese
- 1/2 cup diced onions
- 1 1/2 cups heavy cream
- 4 large eggs
- Salt and pepper to taste
- Pinch of nutmeg (optional)

Instructions:

Preheat the oven to 375°F (190°C).

For the Pie Crust:

- In a food processor, pulse the flour, cold diced butter, and salt until it resembles coarse crumbs.
- Add ice water, one tablespoon at a time, pulsing until the dough just comes together.

- Form the dough into a disk, wrap in plastic wrap, and refrigerate for at least 30 minutes.
- Roll out the chilled dough on a floured surface and place it in a 9-inch pie dish. Trim the edges and prick the bottom with a fork.
- Line the crust with parchment paper and fill it with pie weights or dried beans.
- Blind bake the crust for about 15 minutes. Remove the weights and parchment paper, and bake for an additional 5 minutes until golden brown. Set aside.

For the Filling:

- In a skillet, cook the bacon until crispy. Remove and crumble.
- In the same skillet, sauté the diced onions until softened.
- In a bowl, whisk together the heavy cream, eggs, salt, pepper, and nutmeg (if using).
- Spread the crumbled bacon, sautéed onions, and shredded cheese evenly over the pre-baked pie crust.
- Pour the egg and cream mixture over the filling.

Bake:

- Bake the Quiche Lorraine in the preheated oven for 30-35 minutes or until the center is set and the top is golden brown.
- Allow it to cool for a few minutes before slicing.

Serve Quiche Lorraine warm or at room temperature. Enjoy this classic French dish!

Breakfast Burrito

Ingredients:

- 4 large flour tortillas
- 8 large eggs
- 1/4 cup milk
- Salt and pepper to taste
- 1 tablespoon butter or cooking oil
- 1 cup cooked and diced breakfast sausage or bacon
- 1 cup shredded cheddar cheese
- 1 cup diced tomatoes
- 1/2 cup diced onions
- 1/4 cup chopped fresh cilantro (optional)
- Salsa or hot sauce for serving
- Sour cream for serving (optional)
- Avocado slices for serving (optional)

Instructions:

In a bowl, whisk together the eggs, milk, salt, and pepper.

Heat butter or cooking oil in a skillet over medium heat.

Pour the egg mixture into the skillet and scramble the eggs until cooked through. Remove from heat.

Warm the flour tortillas in a dry skillet or microwave.

Assemble the burritos:
- Place a portion of scrambled eggs in the center of each tortilla.
- Add cooked and diced breakfast sausage or bacon on top of the eggs.

- Sprinkle shredded cheddar cheese over the eggs and meat.
- Add diced tomatoes, onions, and chopped cilantro (if using).

Fold the sides of the tortilla in, then fold the bottom and roll tightly to form the burrito.

Optional: Heat the assembled burritos in a skillet for a few minutes to melt the cheese and warm them through.

Serve the Breakfast Burritos with salsa, hot sauce, sour cream, and avocado slices on the side.

Enjoy your hearty and flavorful Breakfast Burrito! Feel free to customize the ingredients based on your preferences.

Breakfast Quesadilla

Ingredients:

- 4 large flour tortillas
- 1 cup shredded cheddar cheese
- 4 large eggs, scrambled
- Salt and pepper to taste
- 1 cup cooked and crumbled breakfast sausage or bacon
- 1/2 cup diced bell peppers (any color)
- 1/4 cup diced onions
- 1/2 cup diced tomatoes
- Salsa and sour cream for serving
- Chopped fresh cilantro for garnish (optional)
- Avocado slices for serving (optional)

Instructions:

In a skillet over medium heat, cook the breakfast sausage or bacon until browned and cooked through. Remove excess grease if needed.

In the same skillet, add diced bell peppers and onions. Sauté until they are softened.

Push the cooked sausage or bacon, bell peppers, and onions to one side of the skillet.

Pour the scrambled eggs into the empty side of the skillet. Season with salt and pepper. Cook the eggs, stirring gently, until they are just set.

Warm the flour tortillas in a dry skillet or microwave.

Assemble the Quesadillas:

- Place a tortilla on a flat surface.
- Sprinkle a portion of shredded cheddar cheese on one half of the tortilla.

- Add a portion of the scrambled eggs, cooked sausage or bacon, sautéed bell peppers and onions, and diced tomatoes on top of the cheese.
- Fold the other half of the tortilla over the filling to create a half-moon shape.

Repeat the process for the remaining tortillas and filling.

Heat each assembled quesadilla in a skillet over medium heat for a few minutes on each side until the cheese is melted and the tortilla is golden brown.

Slice the quesadillas into wedges and serve with salsa, sour cream, chopped cilantro, and avocado slices on the side.

Enjoy your delicious and satisfying Breakfast Quesadilla! Feel free to customize it with your favorite ingredients.

Breakfast Tacos

Ingredients:

- 8 small corn or flour tortillas
- 6 large eggs
- Salt and pepper to taste
- 1 tablespoon butter or cooking oil
- 1 cup cooked and crumbled breakfast sausage or chorizo
- 1 cup shredded cheddar cheese
- Salsa for serving
- Fresh cilantro, chopped, for garnish (optional)
- Avocado slices for serving (optional)

Instructions:

In a skillet over medium heat, cook the breakfast sausage or chorizo until browned and cooked through. Set aside.

In a bowl, whisk together the eggs, salt, and pepper.

Heat butter or cooking oil in a skillet over medium-low heat.

Pour the whisked eggs into the skillet and cook, stirring gently, until the eggs are just set.

Warm the tortillas in a dry skillet or microwave.

Assemble the Breakfast Tacos:

- Place a portion of scrambled eggs on each tortilla.
- Add a portion of the cooked sausage or chorizo on top of the eggs.
- Sprinkle shredded cheddar cheese over the filling.

Optional: Heat the assembled tacos in the skillet for a minute or until the cheese is melted.

Serve the Breakfast Tacos with salsa on the side.

Garnish with chopped fresh cilantro and avocado slices if desired.

Enjoy your delicious and customizable Breakfast Tacos! Feel free to add your favorite toppings or sauces to enhance the flavor.

Huevos Rancheros

Ingredients:

- 4 large eggs
- 4 small corn or flour tortillas
- 1 cup cooked and seasoned black beans
- 1 cup salsa (homemade or store-bought)
- 1/2 cup diced tomatoes
- 1/2 cup diced onions
- 1/2 cup diced bell peppers (any color)
- 1 cup shredded cheese (cheddar or Mexican blend)
- Fresh cilantro, chopped, for garnish
- Avocado slices for serving
- Lime wedges for serving

Instructions:

Warm the tortillas in a dry skillet or microwave.

In a separate skillet, heat a bit of oil over medium heat. Add diced onions and bell peppers and sauté until softened.

Add the seasoned black beans to the skillet with onions and bell peppers. Cook until heated through.

In another skillet, cook the eggs to your liking. You can fry or scramble them.

Assemble the Huevos Rancheros:
- Place a warmed tortilla on a plate.
- Spread a portion of the black bean mixture over the tortilla.
- Top with the cooked eggs.

- Spoon salsa over the eggs.
- Sprinkle diced tomatoes and shredded cheese on top.

Garnish with chopped cilantro and serve with avocado slices on the side.

Squeeze lime wedges over the top for extra flavor.

Repeat the process for the remaining tortillas.

Enjoy your delicious Huevos Rancheros! This dish is customizable, so feel free to add or adjust ingredients based on your preferences.

Shakshuka

Ingredients:

- 2 tablespoons olive oil
- 1 onion, finely chopped
- 1 bell pepper, diced
- 2 cloves garlic, minced
- 1 teaspoon ground cumin
- 1 teaspoon ground paprika
- 1/2 teaspoon ground cayenne pepper (adjust to taste)
- 1 teaspoon ground coriander
- 1 can (28 ounces) crushed tomatoes
- Salt and pepper to taste
- 4-6 large eggs
- Fresh parsley, chopped, for garnish
- Feta cheese, crumbled, for serving (optional)
- Crusty bread or pita for serving

Instructions:

Heat olive oil in a large skillet or cast-iron pan over medium heat.

Add chopped onions and diced bell pepper. Sauté until the vegetables are softened, about 5 minutes.

Add minced garlic and sauté for an additional 1-2 minutes until fragrant.

Stir in ground cumin, paprika, cayenne pepper, and ground coriander. Cook for another 1-2 minutes to toast the spices.

Pour in the crushed tomatoes and season with salt and pepper. Simmer the sauce for about 10-15 minutes, allowing it to thicken.

Using a spoon, create small wells in the sauce and carefully crack the eggs into the wells. Cover the skillet and let the eggs poach in the sauce for 7-10 minutes, or until the egg whites are set but the yolks are still runny. Adjust the cooking time based on your preference for egg doneness.

Garnish with chopped fresh parsley and crumbled feta cheese (if using).

Serve the Shakshuka hot with crusty bread or pita for dipping.

Enjoy your flavorful and hearty Shakshuka! It's a great dish for breakfast, brunch, or any meal of the day.

Eggs Benedict

Ingredients:

For the Hollandaise Sauce:

- 3 large egg yolks
- 1 tablespoon water
- 1 tablespoon lemon juice
- 1 cup unsalted butter, melted
- Salt and cayenne pepper to taste

For Assembling Eggs Benedict:

- 4 English muffins, split and toasted
- 8 slices Canadian bacon or ham
- 8 large eggs
- Chopped fresh chives or parsley for garnish (optional)
- Salt and pepper to taste

Instructions:

Prepare the Hollandaise Sauce:
- In a heatproof bowl, whisk together egg yolks, water, and lemon juice.
- Place the bowl over a pot of simmering water (double boiler) and whisk continuously until the mixture thickens, about 2-3 minutes.
- Slowly drizzle in the melted butter, whisking constantly, until the sauce is smooth and thick.
- Season with salt and cayenne pepper to taste. Keep the sauce warm.

Poach the Eggs:

- Fill a large saucepan with water and bring it to a gentle simmer.
- Crack each egg into a small bowl or cup.
- Create a gentle whirlpool in the simmering water with a spoon and carefully slide each egg into the center of the whirlpool.
- Poach the eggs for about 3-4 minutes for a soft poach. Adjust the time for your desired level of doneness.
- Remove the poached eggs with a slotted spoon and place them on a plate lined with paper towels to absorb excess water.

Prepare the Canadian Bacon:

- In a skillet, heat Canadian bacon slices until warmed through.

Assemble Eggs Benedict:

- Place a toasted English muffin half on each plate.
- Top each half with a slice of Canadian bacon.
- Gently place a poached egg on top of the Canadian bacon.
- Spoon hollandaise sauce generously over the eggs.
- Garnish with chopped chives or parsley if desired.
- Season with salt and pepper to taste.

Serve:

- Serve Eggs Benedict immediately while warm.

Enjoy your delicious Eggs Benedict for a delightful brunch!

Eggs Florentine

Ingredients:

For the Hollandaise Sauce:

- 3 large egg yolks
- 1 tablespoon water
- 1 tablespoon lemon juice
- 1 cup unsalted butter, melted
- Salt and cayenne pepper to taste

For Assembling Eggs Florentine:

- 4 English muffins, split and toasted
- 2 cups fresh baby spinach
- 1 tablespoon olive oil
- 1 garlic clove, minced (optional)
- 8 large eggs
- Chopped fresh chives or parsley for garnish (optional)
- Salt and pepper to taste

Instructions:

Prepare the Hollandaise Sauce:
- In a heatproof bowl, whisk together egg yolks, water, and lemon juice.
- Place the bowl over a pot of simmering water (double boiler) and whisk continuously until the mixture thickens, about 2-3 minutes.

- Slowly drizzle in the melted butter, whisking constantly, until the sauce is smooth and thick.
- Season with salt and cayenne pepper to taste. Keep the sauce warm.

Sauté the Spinach:

- In a large skillet, heat olive oil over medium heat.
- Add minced garlic (if using) and sauté for about 30 seconds until fragrant.
- Add fresh baby spinach to the skillet and sauté until wilted. Season with salt and pepper to taste.

Poach the Eggs:

- Fill a large saucepan with water and bring it to a gentle simmer.
- Crack each egg into a small bowl or cup.
- Create a gentle whirlpool in the simmering water with a spoon and carefully slide each egg into the center of the whirlpool.
- Poach the eggs for about 3-4 minutes for a soft poach. Adjust the time for your desired level of doneness.
- Remove the poached eggs with a slotted spoon and place them on a plate lined with paper towels to absorb excess water.

Assemble Eggs Florentine:

- Place a toasted English muffin half on each plate.
- Top each half with sautéed spinach.
- Gently place a poached egg on top of the spinach.
- Spoon hollandaise sauce generously over the eggs.
- Garnish with chopped chives or parsley if desired.
- Season with salt and pepper to taste.

Serve:

- Serve Eggs Florentine immediately while warm.

Enjoy your delicious Eggs Florentine for a delightful brunch!

Breakfast Pizza

Ingredients:

- 1 pizza dough (store-bought or homemade)
- 1 cup shredded mozzarella cheese
- 4 large eggs
- Salt and pepper to taste
- 4 slices bacon, cooked and crumbled
- 1/2 cup diced bell peppers (any color)
- 1/4 cup diced onions
- 1/2 cup sliced mushrooms
- 1/2 cup cherry tomatoes, halved
- 1/4 cup chopped fresh parsley or chives for garnish
- Olive oil for drizzling

Instructions:

Preheat the Oven:
- Preheat your oven according to the pizza dough package instructions or the temperature specified in your homemade dough recipe.

Prepare the Pizza Dough:
- Roll out the pizza dough on a floured surface to your desired thickness.

Assemble the Pizza:
- Transfer the rolled-out dough to a pizza stone or baking sheet.
- Sprinkle shredded mozzarella cheese evenly over the pizza dough.

Prepare the Toppings:
- In a skillet, cook bacon until crispy. Crumble the bacon.

- In the same skillet, sauté diced bell peppers, onions, and sliced mushrooms until softened.

Add the Toppings:

- Spread the cooked bacon, sautéed vegetables, and cherry tomato halves over the cheese.

Crack the Eggs:

- Carefully crack each egg onto the pizza, distributing them evenly.

Bake:

- Bake the Breakfast Pizza in the preheated oven according to the pizza dough instructions or until the crust is golden brown, and the eggs are cooked to your liking.

Garnish:

- Remove the pizza from the oven and sprinkle chopped fresh parsley or chives over the top.

Drizzle with Olive Oil:

- Drizzle a little olive oil over the pizza for added flavor.

Serve:

- Slice the Breakfast Pizza and serve it hot.

Feel free to customize the toppings based on your preferences. Breakfast Pizza is a versatile dish, and you can add ingredients like sausage, ham, different cheeses, or even a drizzle of hot sauce for extra kick. Enjoy your delicious Breakfast Pizza!

Breakfast Sandwich

Ingredients:

- 2 English muffins, split and toasted
- 4 large eggs
- Salt and pepper to taste
- 4 slices of Canadian bacon or regular bacon, cooked
- 4 slices of cheese (cheddar, American, Swiss, or your choice)
- Butter for toasting

Optional Toppings:

- Sliced tomatoes
- Avocado slices
- Fresh spinach or arugula
- Hot sauce or ketchup

Instructions:

Prepare the Eggs:
- In a non-stick skillet over medium heat, crack the eggs and cook them to your liking. You can fry them, scramble them, or make a simple omelette.

Season the Eggs:
- Season the eggs with salt and pepper to taste while cooking.

Toast the English Muffins:
- Split the English muffins and toast them to your desired level of crispiness. You can lightly butter them if you like.

Assemble the Breakfast Sandwich:

- Place a slice of cheese on the bottom half of each toasted English muffin.

Add the Eggs:

- Place a cooked egg on top of the cheese.

Add the Meat:

- Add a slice of Canadian bacon or regular bacon on top of the egg.

Optional Toppings:

- Add any optional toppings you prefer, such as sliced tomatoes, avocado slices, fresh spinach, or a drizzle of hot sauce or ketchup.

Complete the Sandwich:

- Top each sandwich with the other half of the toasted English muffin.

Serve:

- Serve the Breakfast Sandwiches hot and enjoy!

Feel free to customize the Breakfast Sandwich with your favorite ingredients. You can also experiment with different cheeses, meats, and toppings to suit your taste. It's a quick and satisfying breakfast option!

Bagel with Cream Cheese and Lox

Ingredients:

- 4 bagels (your choice of flavor)
- 8 ounces cream cheese, softened
- 8 ounces smoked salmon (lox)
- 1 red onion, thinly sliced
- Capers, for garnish
- Fresh dill, for garnish
- Lemon wedges, for serving

Instructions:

Prepare the Bagels:
- Slice the bagels in half.

Spread Cream Cheese:
- Spread a generous layer of softened cream cheese on each half of the bagels.

Add Smoked Salmon:
- Place slices of smoked salmon (lox) on top of the cream cheese. Ensure an even distribution across each bagel.

Top with Onion:
- Add thinly sliced red onion on top of the smoked salmon.

Garnish with Capers:
- Sprinkle capers over the bagels for a burst of briny flavor.

Add Fresh Dill:
- Garnish each bagel with fresh dill. This adds a touch of freshness to the dish.

Serve with Lemon Wedges:

- Serve the Bagels with Cream Cheese and Lox with lemon wedges on the side. Squeezing lemon over the salmon adds brightness to the flavors.

Enjoy:

- Serve the bagels immediately and enjoy your delicious and classic Bagel with Cream Cheese and Lox!

This dish is a popular choice for breakfast or brunch and is often served with additional accompaniments like sliced tomatoes or cucumbers. Customize it based on your preferences and enjoy this delightful combination of flavors!

Smoked Salmon and Avocado Bagel

Ingredients:

- 4 bagels (your choice of flavor)
- 8 ounces cream cheese, softened
- 8 ounces smoked salmon
- 2 ripe avocados, sliced
- 1 tablespoon capers, drained
- 1 lemon, cut into wedges
- Fresh dill, chopped, for garnish
- Salt and black pepper, to taste

Instructions:

Prepare the Bagels:
- Slice the bagels in half.

Spread Cream Cheese:
- Spread a generous layer of softened cream cheese on each half of the bagels.

Layer Smoked Salmon:
- Place slices of smoked salmon on top of the cream cheese. Ensure an even distribution across each bagel.

Add Avocado Slices:
- Arrange slices of ripe avocado over the smoked salmon.

Garnish with Capers:
- Sprinkle capers over the bagels for a burst of briny flavor.

Squeeze Lemon:
- Squeeze lemon wedges over the bagels to add a citrusy zing.

Season with Salt and Pepper:

- Season the bagels with a pinch of salt and black pepper to taste.

Finish with Fresh Dill:

- Garnish each bagel with chopped fresh dill.

Serve:

- Serve the Smoked Salmon and Avocado Bagels immediately and enjoy!

This combination of smoked salmon, creamy avocado, and the freshness of lemon and dill creates a delightful bagel topping. It's a perfect option for a light and flavorful breakfast or brunch. Customize it based on your preferences and enjoy!

Granola with Yogurt

Ingredients:

- 2 cups plain Greek yogurt
- 1 cup granola (store-bought or homemade)
- 1 cup mixed berries (strawberries, blueberries, raspberries)
- 2 tablespoons honey or maple syrup
- 1/4 cup chopped nuts (almonds, walnuts, or your choice)
- 1 teaspoon chia seeds (optional)
- Fresh mint leaves for garnish (optional)

Instructions:

Prepare the Yogurt Base:
- Spoon the Greek yogurt into serving bowls or glasses.

Add Granola:
- Sprinkle a generous amount of granola over the yogurt. Ensure an even distribution.

Top with Mixed Berries:
- Add a layer of mixed berries on top of the granola. You can use fresh or frozen berries.

Drizzle with Honey or Maple Syrup:
- Drizzle honey or maple syrup over the berries for added sweetness.

Sprinkle Chopped Nuts:
- Sprinkle chopped nuts over the top. This adds a delightful crunch.

Optional Chia Seeds:
- If you like, sprinkle chia seeds over the granola for an extra nutritional boost.

Garnish with Fresh Mint (Optional):

- Garnish the yogurt parfait with fresh mint leaves for a burst of freshness.

Serve Immediately:

- Serve the Granola with Yogurt immediately for a delicious and nutritious breakfast or snack.

This recipe is highly customizable, and you can adjust the ingredients based on your preferences. Feel free to add other toppings such as sliced bananas, coconut flakes, or a drizzle of nut butter. Enjoy your wholesome and satisfying granola with yogurt!

Smoothie Bowl

Ingredients:

For the Smoothie Base:

- 1 frozen banana, sliced
- 1 cup frozen mixed berries (strawberries, blueberries, raspberries)
- 1/2 cup Greek yogurt
- 1/2 cup milk (dairy or plant-based)
- 1 tablespoon honey or maple syrup (optional for sweetness)
- 1 tablespoon chia seeds (optional)

Toppings:

- Sliced fresh fruits (banana, berries, kiwi)
- Granola
- Nuts and seeds (almonds, chia seeds, pumpkin seeds)
- Coconut flakes
- Drizzle of honey or nut butter (optional)

Instructions:

Prepare the Smoothie Base:
- In a blender, combine the frozen banana, frozen mixed berries, Greek yogurt, milk, honey or maple syrup (if using), and chia seeds (if using).
- Blend until smooth and creamy. You may need to stop and scrape down the sides of the blender to ensure everything is well mixed.

Assemble the Smoothie Bowl:

- Pour the smoothie into a bowl.

Add Toppings:

- Arrange your favorite toppings on the smoothie bowl. Get creative with the combination of fruits, granola, nuts, and seeds.

Drizzle with Honey or Nut Butter (Optional):

- If you like, drizzle a little honey or nut butter over the toppings for added sweetness and flavor.

Serve Immediately:

- Enjoy your delicious and visually appealing Smoothie Bowl immediately!

Feel free to customize your Smoothie Bowl with a variety of toppings based on your preferences. Smoothie Bowls are not only tasty but also a great way to incorporate a variety of nutrients into your breakfast or snack. Enjoy!

Acai Bowl

Ingredients:

For the Acai Bowl Base:

- 2 frozen Acai Berry Packets (unsweetened)
- 1 frozen banana, sliced
- 1/2 cup frozen mixed berries (strawberries, blueberries, raspberries)
- 1/2 cup almond milk or coconut water
- 1 tablespoon honey or maple syrup (optional for sweetness)
- 1 tablespoon chia seeds (optional)

Toppings:

- Sliced fresh fruits (banana, berries, kiwi)
- Granola
- Nuts and seeds (almonds, chia seeds, pumpkin seeds)
- Coconut flakes
- Drizzle of honey or nut butter (optional)

Instructions:

Prepare the Acai Bowl Base:
- Run the frozen Acai Berry Packets under warm water for a few seconds to break them into chunks.
- In a blender, combine the frozen Acai chunks, frozen banana, frozen mixed berries, almond milk or coconut water, honey or maple syrup (if using), and chia seeds (if using).

- Blend until you achieve a smooth and thick consistency. You may need to stop and scrape down the sides of the blender to ensure everything is well mixed.

Assemble the Acai Bowl:

- Pour the Acai smoothie into a bowl.

Add Toppings:

- Arrange your favorite toppings on the Acai Bowl. Use a combination of sliced fresh fruits, granola, nuts, seeds, and coconut flakes.

Drizzle with Honey or Nut Butter (Optional):

- If you like, drizzle a little honey or nut butter over the toppings for added sweetness and flavor.

Serve Immediately:

- Enjoy your refreshing and nutritious Acai Bowl immediately!

Acai Bowls are not only delicious but also packed with antioxidants and nutrients. Customize your bowl with a variety of toppings to suit your taste preferences. Enjoy!

Chia Seed Pudding

Ingredients:

- 1/4 cup chia seeds
- 1 cup milk (dairy or plant-based)
- 1 tablespoon honey or maple syrup (adjust to taste)
- 1/2 teaspoon vanilla extract
- Fresh fruits, berries, or nuts for topping (optional)

Instructions:

Mix Ingredients:

- In a bowl or jar, combine the chia seeds, milk, honey or maple syrup, and vanilla extract. Stir well to make sure the chia seeds are evenly distributed.

Stir Again:

- After about 5 minutes, stir the mixture again to prevent the chia seeds from clumping together.

Refrigerate:

- Cover the bowl or jar and refrigerate the mixture for at least 2-3 hours, or preferably overnight. This allows the chia seeds to absorb the liquid and create a pudding-like consistency.

Check and Stir:

- After the initial refrigeration time, check the pudding. If it's too thick, you can add a bit more milk and stir until you achieve your desired consistency.

Serve:

- Once the chia seed pudding has reached the desired thickness, you can serve it as is or layer it with fresh fruits, berries, or nuts.

Top with Fresh Fruits (Optional):

- Add your favorite fresh fruits, berries, or nuts on top for added flavor and texture.

Enjoy:

- Enjoy your Chia Seed Pudding as a healthy and satisfying breakfast, snack, or dessert!

Chia Seed Pudding is highly versatile, and you can customize it by adding flavors such as cinnamon, cocoa powder, or almond extract. Experiment with different toppings and variations to suit your taste preferences.

Breakfast Casserole

Ingredients:

- 8 large eggs
- 1 cup milk
- 1 teaspoon Dijon mustard
- Salt and pepper to taste
- 6 slices bread, cubed (day-old or slightly stale works well)
- 1 lb (450g) breakfast sausage, cooked and crumbled
- 1 cup shredded cheddar cheese (or your favorite cheese)
- 1 cup diced bell peppers (any color)
- 1 cup diced onions
- 1 cup sliced mushrooms
- 1 cup cherry tomatoes, halved
- 2 tablespoons chopped fresh parsley (optional)

Instructions:

Preheat the Oven:
- Preheat your oven to 350°F (175°C). Grease a 9x13-inch baking dish.

Prepare the Egg Mixture:
- In a large bowl, whisk together the eggs, milk, Dijon mustard, salt, and pepper.

Assemble the Casserole:
- Place the cubed bread in the prepared baking dish.
- Sprinkle the cooked and crumbled breakfast sausage over the bread.
- Add the shredded cheese, diced bell peppers, onions, mushrooms, and cherry tomatoes evenly over the bread and sausage.

Pour the Egg Mixture:

- Pour the whisked egg mixture evenly over the ingredients in the baking dish. Ensure that the eggs coat everything.

Let It Soak:

- Allow the casserole to sit for about 10-15 minutes, giving the bread a chance to soak up the egg mixture.

Bake:

- Bake in the preheated oven for 40-45 minutes or until the top is golden brown and the center is set.

Check for Doneness:

- To check for doneness, insert a knife into the center. If it comes out clean, the casserole is ready.

Garnish (Optional):

- Sprinkle chopped fresh parsley over the casserole for a pop of color and freshness.

Serve:

- Allow the casserole to cool slightly before slicing and serving.

Enjoy your hearty and flavorful Breakfast Casserole! This recipe is versatile, so feel free to customize it with your favorite ingredients like spinach, bacon, or different types of cheese.

Hash Browns

Ingredients:

- 4 medium russet potatoes, peeled and grated
- 1 small onion, finely diced
- 2 tablespoons all-purpose flour
- 1 teaspoon salt
- 1/2 teaspoon black pepper
- Vegetable oil for frying

Instructions:

Grate the Potatoes:
- Peel the potatoes and grate them using a box grater or a food processor. Place the grated potatoes in a clean kitchen towel or cheesecloth and squeeze out any excess moisture.

Prepare the Onion:
- Finely dice the small onion.

Combine Ingredients:
- In a large bowl, combine the grated potatoes, diced onion, all-purpose flour, salt, and black pepper. Mix well to ensure even distribution of ingredients.

Shape into Patties:
- Take handfuls of the mixture and shape them into flat, round patties. Press them together firmly to help hold their shape.

Heat the Oil:
- In a large skillet, heat vegetable oil over medium-high heat. Make sure there's enough oil to cover the bottom of the skillet.

Fry the Hash Browns:
- Carefully place the hash brown patties in the hot oil, leaving some space between each one. Fry until the bottom is golden brown and crispy.

Flip and Cook:
- Use a spatula to flip the hash browns and cook the other side until golden brown and crispy. This usually takes about 5-7 minutes per side.

Drain Excess Oil:
- Once cooked, transfer the hash browns to a plate lined with paper towels to drain any excess oil.

Serve Warm:
- Serve the hash browns warm with your favorite breakfast items or as a side dish.

Enjoy your homemade Hash Browns! They pair well with eggs, bacon, or as a side for breakfast or brunch. Feel free to customize the recipe by adding herbs, spices, or cheese to the potato mixture.

Sweet Potato Hash

Ingredients:

- 2 medium sweet potatoes, peeled and diced into small cubes
- 1 bell pepper, diced
- 1 red onion, diced
- 2 cloves garlic, minced
- 2 tablespoons olive oil
- 1 teaspoon ground cumin
- 1 teaspoon smoked paprika
- Salt and pepper to taste
- Optional: 1/2 teaspoon chili powder for some heat
- Fresh parsley or cilantro for garnish (optional)
- Fried or poached eggs for serving (optional)

Instructions:

Preheat the Pan:
- Heat olive oil in a large skillet or frying pan over medium heat.

Sauté Vegetables:
- Add the diced sweet potatoes, bell pepper, and red onion to the pan. Sauté for about 10-15 minutes or until the sweet potatoes are tender, stirring occasionally.

Add Garlic and Spices:
- Add minced garlic, ground cumin, smoked paprika, salt, pepper, and optional chili powder to the pan. Stir to coat the vegetables evenly with the spices. Cook for an additional 2-3 minutes.

Crisp Edges:

- Let the sweet potato mixture sit without stirring for a few minutes to allow the edges to crisp up. Then, stir and let it sit again for crisping.

Check for Doneness:

- Taste a piece of sweet potato to ensure it's cooked through and seasoned to your liking. Adjust seasoning if needed.

Garnish:

- Garnish the sweet potato hash with fresh parsley or cilantro if desired.

Serve:

- Serve the Sweet Potato Hash warm as a side dish or topped with fried or poached eggs for a complete and satisfying meal.

Enjoy your flavorful and nutritious Sweet Potato Hash! This dish is not only delicious but also a great option for a hearty and wholesome breakfast or brunch.

Bacon and Egg Muffins

Ingredients:

- 6 large eggs
- 6 slices bacon
- 1 cup shredded cheddar cheese
- Salt and pepper to taste
- Fresh chives or parsley for garnish (optional)
- Cooking spray or butter for greasing muffin tin

Instructions:

Preheat the Oven:
- Preheat your oven to 375°F (190°C). Grease a muffin tin with cooking spray or butter.

Cook Bacon:
- In a skillet over medium heat, cook the bacon until it's crispy. Remove from the skillet and place it on paper towels to absorb excess grease. Once cooled, crumble the bacon into small pieces.

Prepare Muffin Tin:
- Place a small amount of crumbled bacon at the bottom of each muffin cup.

Crack Eggs:
- Crack one egg into each muffin cup on top of the bacon.

Season:
- Season each egg with a pinch of salt and pepper to taste.

Top with Cheese:
- Sprinkle shredded cheddar cheese on top of each egg.

Bake:

- Bake in the preheated oven for about 15-20 minutes or until the eggs are set to your liking.

Garnish (Optional):

- Garnish with fresh chives or parsley if desired.

Serve Warm:

- Allow the Bacon and Egg Muffins to cool for a few minutes before carefully removing them from the muffin tin. Serve warm.

These Bacon and Egg Muffins make a delicious and convenient breakfast or brunch. You can also customize them by adding ingredients like diced tomatoes, spinach, or bell peppers to the muffin cups before baking. Enjoy!

Sausage and Cheese Biscuits

Ingredients:

- 1 pound (16 ounces) breakfast sausage
- 2 cups all-purpose flour
- 1 tablespoon baking powder
- 1/2 teaspoon baking soda
- 1/2 teaspoon salt
- 1/2 cup unsalted butter, cold and cut into small cubes
- 1 cup shredded cheddar cheese
- 3/4 cup buttermilk
- Optional: 1/4 teaspoon garlic powder for added flavor

Instructions:

Preheat the Oven:
- Preheat your oven to 425°F (220°C). Line a baking sheet with parchment paper.

Cook Sausage:
- In a skillet over medium heat, cook the breakfast sausage until browned and cooked through. Break it into crumbles with a spatula. Once cooked, remove excess grease and set aside to cool.

Prepare Dry Ingredients:
- In a large bowl, whisk together the flour, baking powder, baking soda, salt, and optional garlic powder.

Add Butter:

- Add the cold, cubed butter to the dry ingredients. Use a pastry cutter or your fingers to work the butter into the flour until the mixture resembles coarse crumbs.

Add Sausage and Cheese:

- Add the cooked sausage crumbles and shredded cheddar cheese to the flour mixture. Mix until evenly distributed.

Add Buttermilk:

- Pour in the buttermilk and stir until just combined. Do not overmix; the dough should be slightly sticky.

Shape and Cut:

- Turn the dough out onto a floured surface. Pat it into a rectangle, about 1/2 to 3/4 inch thick. Use a biscuit cutter or a round glass to cut out biscuits.

Bake:

- Place the biscuits on the prepared baking sheet and bake in the preheated oven for 12-15 minutes or until golden brown.

Serve Warm:

- Allow the Sausage and Cheese Biscuits to cool for a few minutes before serving. Enjoy them warm!

These biscuits are perfect for a savory breakfast or brunch. You can also make them in advance and reheat them for a quick and delicious meal. Feel free to customize the recipe by adding herbs or spices to the dough for extra flavor.

Cinnamon Rolls

Ingredients:

For the Dough:

- 1 cup warm milk (110°F/43°C)
- 2 1/2 teaspoons active dry yeast
- 1/2 cup granulated sugar
- 1/3 cup unsalted butter, melted
- 1 teaspoon salt
- 2 large eggs
- 4 cups all-purpose flour

For the Filling:

- 1/2 cup unsalted butter, softened
- 1 cup packed brown sugar
- 2 tablespoons ground cinnamon

For the Cream Cheese Frosting:

- 4 ounces cream cheese, softened
- 1/4 cup unsalted butter, softened
- 1 cup powdered sugar
- 1/2 teaspoon vanilla extract

Instructions:

1. Activate the Yeast:

- In a bowl, combine warm milk and yeast. Let it sit for about 5 minutes until it becomes frothy.

2. Make the Dough:

    - In a large mixing bowl, combine the activated yeast mixture, sugar, melted butter, salt, and eggs. Mix well.
    - Gradually add in the flour, one cup at a time, stirring well after each addition. Continue until the dough forms.

3. Knead the Dough:

    - Turn the dough out onto a floured surface and knead for about 5-7 minutes until it becomes smooth and elastic.

4. Let the Dough Rise:

    - Place the dough in a greased bowl, cover it with a clean kitchen towel, and let it rise in a warm place for about 1-1.5 hours or until it doubles in size.

5. Roll Out the Dough:

    - Once the dough has risen, roll it out on a floured surface into a large rectangle.

6. Make the Filling:

    - Spread the softened butter over the rolled-out dough.
    - In a small bowl, mix together brown sugar and ground cinnamon. Sprinkle this mixture evenly over the buttered dough.

7. Roll the Dough:

- Starting from one long edge, tightly roll the dough into a log shape.

8. Cut into Rolls:

- Using a sharp knife, cut the rolled dough into 12 equal pieces.

9. Place in a Pan:

- Arrange the cut cinnamon rolls in a greased baking pan, leaving a little space between each.

10. Let Rise Again:

- Cover the pan with a towel and let the rolls rise for an additional 30-45 minutes.

11. Preheat the Oven:

- Preheat your oven to 375°F (190°C).

12. Bake:

- Bake the cinnamon rolls in the preheated oven for 20-25 minutes or until they are golden brown.

13. Make the Frosting:

- While the rolls are baking, prepare the cream cheese frosting. In a bowl, beat together softened cream cheese, softened butter, powdered sugar, and vanilla extract until smooth.

14. Frost the Rolls:

- Once the cinnamon rolls are out of the oven, let them cool slightly, and then spread the cream cheese frosting over the warm rolls.

15. Serve and Enjoy:

- Serve the cinnamon rolls warm and enjoy!

These homemade cinnamon rolls are a delightful treat, especially when served fresh out of the oven. Enjoy the delicious aroma and the soft, gooey centers!

Breakfast Sliders

Ingredients:

For the Sliders:

- 12 small slider rolls or dinner rolls
- 6 large eggs
- 6 slices of bacon, cooked until crispy
- 6 slices of cheese (cheddar, Swiss, or your choice)
- Salt and pepper to taste
- Butter for brushing

For Optional Toppings:

- Sliced tomatoes
- Avocado slices
- Fresh spinach or arugula

Instructions:

Preheat the Oven:
- Preheat your oven to 350°F (175°C).

Prepare the Eggs:
- In a bowl, whisk the eggs and season with salt and pepper. Cook the eggs as scrambled eggs in a skillet over medium heat until just set.

Slice the Rolls:
- If the slider rolls are not pre-sliced, use a serrated knife to carefully slice them in half horizontally, keeping the top and bottom halves intact.

Assemble the Sliders:
- Place the bottom half of the slider rolls in a baking dish.
- Layer the cooked scrambled eggs over the bottom half of the rolls.

Add Bacon and Cheese:
- Place a slice of bacon on top of the eggs on each roll.
- Add a slice of cheese on top of the bacon.

Optional Toppings:
- Add any optional toppings you prefer, such as sliced tomatoes, avocado slices, or fresh spinach.

Top with the Other Half:
- Place the top half of the slider rolls over the fillings to create sandwiches.

Brush with Butter:
- Melt some butter and brush it over the tops of the sliders for a golden finish.

Bake:
- Bake the assembled sliders in the preheated oven for about 10-12 minutes or until the cheese is melted, and the tops are golden.

Serve Warm:
- Remove from the oven, let them cool for a minute, and then use a knife to separate the sliders. Serve warm.

Enjoy your delicious Breakfast Sliders! These sliders are customizable, so feel free to add or modify ingredients based on your preferences. They make for a convenient and tasty breakfast or brunch option.

Spinach and Cheese Strata

Ingredients:

- 8 cups French bread, cubed (day-old or slightly stale works well)
- 2 cups fresh spinach, chopped
- 1 1/2 cups shredded sharp cheddar cheese
- 1/2 cup grated Parmesan cheese
- 1/2 cup diced cooked ham or cooked and crumbled bacon (optional)
- 8 large eggs
- 2 1/2 cups milk
- 1 teaspoon Dijon mustard
- 1/2 teaspoon salt
- 1/4 teaspoon black pepper
- 1/4 teaspoon nutmeg (optional)

Instructions:

Prepare the Bread Cubes:
- Spread the cubed French bread in a greased 9x13-inch baking dish.

Layer with Spinach and Cheese:
- Sprinkle the chopped spinach, shredded cheddar cheese, Parmesan cheese, and diced ham or bacon (if using) over the bread cubes.

Prepare the Egg Mixture:
- In a bowl, whisk together the eggs, milk, Dijon mustard, salt, pepper, and nutmeg (if using).

Pour Over the Bread:

- Pour the egg mixture evenly over the bread, ensuring that it coats all the ingredients.

Press Down:
- Press down on the bread slightly to help it absorb the liquid.

Cover and Refrigerate:
- Cover the baking dish with plastic wrap and refrigerate for at least 4 hours or overnight. This allows the bread to soak up the egg mixture.

Preheat the Oven:
- Preheat your oven to 350°F (175°C).

Bake:
- Remove the strata from the refrigerator and let it come to room temperature for about 15 minutes. Bake in the preheated oven for 45-55 minutes or until the top is golden brown and the center is set.

Check for Doneness:
- To check for doneness, insert a knife into the center. If it comes out clean, the strata is ready.

Serve Warm:
- Let the Spinach and Cheese Strata cool for a few minutes before slicing. Serve warm.

Enjoy this flavorful and satisfying Spinach and Cheese Strata for brunch or breakfast. It's a make-ahead dish that's perfect for entertaining or a relaxed weekend morning.

Baked Eggs in Tomato Sauce

Ingredients:

- 2 tablespoons olive oil
- 1 onion, finely chopped
- 2 bell peppers, diced (any color)
- 3 cloves garlic, minced
- 1 teaspoon ground cumin
- 1 teaspoon ground paprika
- 1/2 teaspoon cayenne pepper (adjust to taste)
- 1 can (28 ounces) crushed tomatoes
- Salt and pepper to taste
- 4-6 large eggs
- Fresh parsley or cilantro for garnish
- Feta cheese or goat cheese for serving (optional)
- Crusty bread for serving

Instructions:

Preheat the Oven:

- Preheat your oven to 375°F (190°C).

Sauté Vegetables:

- In an oven-safe skillet, heat olive oil over medium heat. Add chopped onions and diced bell peppers. Sauté until softened, about 5-7 minutes.

Add Garlic and Spices:

- Add minced garlic, ground cumin, ground paprika, and cayenne pepper to the skillet. Stir and cook for an additional 1-2 minutes until fragrant.

Pour in Crushed Tomatoes:

- Pour in the crushed tomatoes, season with salt and pepper, and stir well. Allow the mixture to simmer for 10-15 minutes until the sauce thickens slightly.

Make Wells for Eggs:

- Create wells in the tomato sauce using a spoon. Crack one egg into each well, spacing them evenly.

Bake in the Oven:

- Transfer the skillet to the preheated oven and bake for about 12-15 minutes or until the egg whites are set, but the yolks are still runny.

Garnish:

- Remove from the oven, and garnish with fresh parsley or cilantro.

Serve Warm:

- Serve the Baked Eggs in Tomato Sauce immediately, with optional crumbled feta or goat cheese on top. Provide crusty bread for dipping.

Enjoy this flavorful and satisfying Baked Eggs in Tomato Sauce for a delightful brunch or breakfast. It's a dish that's both comforting and full of rich flavors.

Breakfast Stir-Fry

Ingredients:

- 1 tablespoon vegetable oil
- 1 small onion, thinly sliced
- 1 bell pepper, thinly sliced (any color)
- 1 cup sliced mushrooms
- 2 cups baby spinach or kale, washed and chopped
- 4 eggs
- Salt and pepper to taste
- 1 teaspoon soy sauce (optional)
- 1 teaspoon hot sauce or Sriracha (optional)
- Chopped green onions for garnish
- Cooked rice or quinoa for serving

Instructions:

Prep Ingredients:
- Wash and chop all the vegetables. Crack the eggs into a bowl and beat them.

Heat the Pan:
- Heat vegetable oil in a large skillet or wok over medium-high heat.

Sauté Vegetables:
- Add the sliced onion, bell pepper, and mushrooms to the pan. Stir-fry for 3-4 minutes until the vegetables are tender-crisp.

Add Spinach:
- Add the chopped spinach or kale to the pan. Stir until the greens are wilted.

Push Vegetables to the Side:

- Push the cooked vegetables to one side of the pan, creating space for the eggs.

Scramble Eggs:

- Pour the beaten eggs into the empty side of the pan. Allow them to sit for a moment, then gently scramble them with a spatula until just set.

Combine and Season:

- Mix the scrambled eggs with the sautéed vegetables. Season the stir-fry with salt and pepper to taste.

Add Soy Sauce and Hot Sauce (Optional):

- If desired, add soy sauce for a savory flavor and hot sauce or Sriracha for a bit of heat. Toss everything together.

Garnish and Serve:

- Garnish the Breakfast Stir-Fry with chopped green onions. Serve over cooked rice or quinoa.

Enjoy your delicious and nutritious Breakfast Stir-Fry! This versatile dish allows you to customize the vegetables and seasonings based on your preferences. It's a great way to start your day with a flavorful and satisfying meal.

Breakfast Skewers

Ingredients:

- 8 slices of cooked bacon, cut into bite-sized pieces
- 8 cherry tomatoes
- 8 mini mozzarella balls (bocconcini)
- 1 avocado, diced
- 8 small pieces of whole grain bread, toasted
- Fresh basil leaves
- Balsamic glaze for drizzling (optional)
- Salt and pepper to taste

Instructions:

Prepare Ingredients:
- Cook the bacon until crispy and cut it into bite-sized pieces. Toast the whole grain bread.

Assemble Skewers:
- Take a skewer and thread a piece of bacon, followed by a cherry tomato, a piece of toasted bread, a mini mozzarella ball, a piece of avocado, and a fresh basil leaf. Repeat until all skewers are assembled.

Arrange on a Platter:
- Arrange the breakfast skewers on a serving platter.

Season and Drizzle:
- Sprinkle a bit of salt and pepper over the skewers. Optionally, drizzle balsamic glaze over the top for extra flavor.

Serve:

- Serve the Breakfast Skewers as a fun and visually appealing breakfast or brunch option.

These Breakfast Skewers are not only delicious but also offer a variety of flavors and textures. They make for a great addition to brunch gatherings or a creative way to enjoy a balanced breakfast. Feel free to customize the ingredients based on your preferences!

Pumpkin Pancakes

Ingredients:

- 1 cup all-purpose flour
- 2 tablespoons brown sugar
- 1 teaspoon baking powder
- 1/2 teaspoon baking soda
- 1/2 teaspoon ground cinnamon
- 1/4 teaspoon ground nutmeg
- 1/4 teaspoon ground ginger
- 1/4 teaspoon salt
- 3/4 cup buttermilk
- 1/2 cup pumpkin puree
- 1 large egg
- 2 tablespoons unsalted butter, melted
- 1 teaspoon vanilla extract
- Cooking spray or additional butter for greasing the griddle

Instructions:

Preheat the Griddle:
- Preheat a griddle or non-stick skillet over medium-high heat.

Mix Dry Ingredients:
- In a large bowl, whisk together the flour, brown sugar, baking powder, baking soda, cinnamon, nutmeg, ginger, and salt.

Prepare Wet Ingredients:

- In another bowl, whisk together the buttermilk, pumpkin puree, egg, melted butter, and vanilla extract.

Combine Wet and Dry Ingredients:

- Pour the wet ingredients into the dry ingredients and stir until just combined. Be careful not to overmix; it's okay if there are a few lumps.

Grease the Griddle:

- Lightly grease the griddle with cooking spray or butter.

Cook the Pancakes:

- Pour 1/4 cup portions of batter onto the griddle. Cook until bubbles form on the surface of the pancakes and the edges start to look set.

Flip and Cook:

- Flip the pancakes and cook the other side until golden brown.

Repeat:

- Repeat the process with the remaining batter, adding more cooking spray or butter to the griddle as needed.

Serve Warm:

- Serve the Pumpkin Pancakes warm with your favorite toppings, such as maple syrup, whipped cream, or chopped nuts.

Enjoy these fluffy and flavorful Pumpkin Pancakes, perfect for a cozy fall breakfast or brunch!

Apple Cinnamon Oatmeal

Ingredients:

- 1 cup old-fashioned oats
- 2 cups milk (dairy or plant-based)
- 1 medium-sized apple, peeled, cored, and diced
- 1 tablespoon unsalted butter
- 1-2 tablespoons brown sugar (adjust to taste)
- 1/2 teaspoon ground cinnamon
- 1/4 teaspoon vanilla extract
- Pinch of salt
- Optional toppings: chopped nuts, raisins, sliced banana, or a drizzle of honey

Instructions:

Prepare the Apple:

- In a medium-sized saucepan, melt the butter over medium heat. Add the diced apple and cook for 2-3 minutes until slightly softened.

Add Oats and Liquid:

- Add the old-fashioned oats to the saucepan and stir to combine with the apples. Pour in the milk.

Season and Simmer:

- Stir in the brown sugar, ground cinnamon, vanilla extract, and a pinch of salt. Bring the mixture to a simmer over medium heat.

Cook Oatmeal:

- Reduce the heat to low and simmer the oatmeal, stirring occasionally, for about 5-7 minutes or until the oats are cooked to your desired consistency.

Check and Adjust:

- Taste the oatmeal and adjust the sweetness and cinnamon level according to your preference.

Serve:

- Once the oatmeal is cooked, remove the saucepan from heat. Serve the Apple Cinnamon Oatmeal warm.

Add Toppings (Optional):

- Customize your oatmeal by adding optional toppings such as chopped nuts, raisins, sliced banana, or a drizzle of honey.

Enjoy your warm and comforting bowl of Apple Cinnamon Oatmeal, a perfect breakfast option for a cozy and satisfying start to your day!

Peanut Butter Banana Toast

Ingredients:

- 2 slices of whole-grain bread (or your preferred bread)
- 2 tablespoons creamy peanut butter
- 1 ripe banana, sliced
- Honey for drizzling (optional)
- Chia seeds or sliced strawberries for garnish (optional)

Instructions:

Toast the Bread:
- Toast the slices of bread to your desired level of crispiness.

Spread Peanut Butter:
- Once toasted, spread a generous layer of creamy peanut butter evenly over each slice of bread.

Add Banana Slices:
- Arrange the sliced bananas on top of the peanut butter, covering the entire surface.

Drizzle Honey (Optional):
- If you like, drizzle a bit of honey over the banana slices for added sweetness.

Garnish (Optional):
- Sprinkle chia seeds or add sliced strawberries on top for extra flavor and texture.

Serve and Enjoy:
- Serve the Peanut Butter Banana Toast immediately while it's warm.

This Peanut Butter Banana Toast is a quick and tasty breakfast or snack option that combines the creaminess of peanut butter with the natural sweetness of ripe bananas. It's a classic and satisfying combination!

Breakfast Stuffed Peppers

Ingredients:

- 4 large bell peppers, halved and seeds removed
- 1 tablespoon olive oil
- 1/2 cup onion, finely chopped
- 1/2 cup bell pepper, finely chopped
- 1/2 cup cherry tomatoes, diced
- 1 cup cooked quinoa or cooked breakfast potatoes
- 1 cup cooked breakfast sausage or bacon, crumbled
- 4 large eggs
- Salt and pepper to taste
- Fresh herbs (such as parsley or chives) for garnish

Instructions:

Preheat the Oven:

- Preheat your oven to 375°F (190°C).

Prepare the Peppers:

- Cut the bell peppers in half lengthwise, removing the seeds and membranes. Place the pepper halves in a baking dish.

Sauté Vegetables:

- In a skillet, heat olive oil over medium heat. Add chopped onions, chopped bell pepper, and diced cherry tomatoes. Sauté until the vegetables are softened.

Combine Ingredients:

- In a large bowl, combine the cooked vegetables, cooked quinoa or breakfast potatoes, and crumbled breakfast sausage or bacon. Mix well.

Stuff Peppers:

- Spoon the mixture into each bell pepper half, creating a well in the center for the egg.

Crack Eggs:

- Crack one egg into each pepper half, on top of the stuffing.

Season:

- Sprinkle salt and pepper over each egg and the stuffed peppers.

Bake:

- Bake in the preheated oven for 20-25 minutes or until the eggs are cooked to your desired doneness.

Garnish:

- Garnish the Breakfast Stuffed Peppers with fresh herbs, such as parsley or chives.

Serve Warm:

- Serve the stuffed peppers warm, and enjoy your delicious and nutritious breakfast!

These Breakfast Stuffed Peppers are a creative and wholesome way to start your day. They are customizable, so feel free to add ingredients like cheese or avocado for extra flavor.

Greek Frittata

Ingredients:

- 8 large eggs
- 1/4 cup milk
- 1 tablespoon olive oil
- 1 small red onion, finely chopped
- 1 bell pepper (any color), diced
- 1 cup cherry tomatoes, halved
- 1 cup fresh spinach, chopped
- 1/2 cup feta cheese, crumbled
- 1 teaspoon dried oregano
- Salt and pepper to taste
- Fresh parsley for garnish (optional)

Instructions:

Preheat the Oven:
- Preheat your oven broiler.

Whisk Eggs:
- In a bowl, whisk together the eggs and milk until well combined. Season with salt and pepper.

Sauté Vegetables:
- Heat olive oil in an oven-safe skillet over medium heat. Add the chopped red onion and diced bell pepper. Sauté until softened.

Add Spinach and Tomatoes:

- Add the chopped spinach and halved cherry tomatoes to the skillet. Cook for an additional 2-3 minutes until the spinach wilts and the tomatoes soften.

Pour Egg Mixture:

- Pour the whisked egg mixture evenly over the sautéed vegetables in the skillet.

Sprinkle Feta and Oregano:

- Sprinkle crumbled feta cheese and dried oregano over the eggs.

Cook on Stovetop:

- Allow the frittata to cook on the stovetop for about 2-3 minutes, lifting the edges with a spatula to let the uncooked eggs flow underneath.

Broil in the Oven:

- Transfer the skillet to the preheated oven and broil for 3-5 minutes or until the top is set, and the edges are golden brown. Keep a close eye to prevent burning.

Garnish and Serve:

- Remove from the oven, garnish with fresh parsley if desired, and let it cool for a minute. Slice and serve.

Serve Warm:

- Serve the Greek Frittata warm as a delicious and protein-packed breakfast or brunch option.

This Greek Frittata is filled with Mediterranean flavors and is a versatile dish that can be enjoyed for any meal. Feel free to customize it by adding olives, sun-dried tomatoes, or other favorite Greek ingredients.

Raspberry Almond Scones

Ingredients:

- 2 cups all-purpose flour
- 1/3 cup granulated sugar
- 1 tablespoon baking powder
- 1/2 teaspoon salt
- 1/2 cup unsalted butter, cold and cut into small cubes
- 1/2 cup sliced almonds
- 1 cup fresh raspberries
- 2/3 cup milk (plus extra for brushing)
- 1 teaspoon almond extract
- 1 teaspoon vanilla extract
- Powdered sugar for dusting (optional)

Instructions:

Preheat the Oven:
- Preheat your oven to 425°F (220°C). Line a baking sheet with parchment paper.

Mix Dry Ingredients:
- In a large bowl, whisk together the all-purpose flour, granulated sugar, baking powder, and salt.

Add Cold Butter:
- Add the cold, cubed butter to the flour mixture. Use a pastry cutter or your fingers to work the butter into the flour until the mixture resembles coarse crumbs.

Add Almonds and Raspberries:

- Stir in the sliced almonds. Gently fold in the fresh raspberries, being careful not to crush them.

Combine Wet Ingredients:

- In a separate bowl, mix together the milk, almond extract, and vanilla extract.

Mix Wet and Dry Ingredients:

- Pour the wet ingredients into the dry ingredients. Stir until just combined; do not overmix.

Shape the Dough:

- Turn the dough out onto a floured surface. Pat it into a circle about 1 inch thick.

Cut into Wedges:

- Use a sharp knife to cut the dough into 8 wedges.

Transfer to Baking Sheet:

- Place the wedges on the prepared baking sheet, leaving some space between each.

Brush with Milk:

- Brush the tops of the scones with a little milk.

Bake:

- Bake in the preheated oven for 12-15 minutes or until the scones are golden brown.

Cool and Dust with Powdered Sugar:

- Allow the Raspberry Almond Scones to cool on a wire rack. Optionally, dust with powdered sugar before serving.

Enjoy these delicious and tender Raspberry Almond Scones with a cup of tea or coffee for a delightful treat!

Banana Nut Muffins

Ingredients:

- 2 to 3 ripe bananas, mashed (about 1 cup)
- 1/2 cup unsalted butter, melted
- 1 teaspoon vanilla extract
- 1/2 cup granulated sugar
- 1/4 cup brown sugar, packed
- 1 large egg
- 1 1/2 cups all-purpose flour
- 1 teaspoon baking soda
- 1/2 teaspoon baking powder
- 1/4 teaspoon salt
- 1/2 cup chopped nuts (walnuts or pecans), optional

Instructions:

Preheat the Oven:
- Preheat your oven to 350°F (175°C). Line a muffin tin with paper liners or grease the muffin cups.

Mash Bananas:
- In a mixing bowl, mash the ripe bananas with a fork or potato masher until smooth.

Mix Wet Ingredients:
- Add melted butter, vanilla extract, granulated sugar, brown sugar, and the egg to the mashed bananas. Mix until well combined.

Combine Dry Ingredients:

- In a separate bowl, whisk together the all-purpose flour, baking soda, baking powder, and salt.

Combine Wet and Dry Mixtures:

- Add the dry ingredients to the wet ingredients and stir until just combined. Do not overmix.

Add Nuts (Optional):

- If using nuts, fold in the chopped nuts into the batter.

Fill Muffin Cups:

- Spoon the batter into the muffin cups, filling each about 2/3 to 3/4 full.

Bake:

- Bake in the preheated oven for 18-20 minutes or until a toothpick inserted into the center comes out clean.

Cool:

- Allow the Banana Nut Muffins to cool in the muffin tin for a few minutes before transferring them to a wire rack to cool completely.

Serve and Enjoy:

- Serve the muffins warm or at room temperature. Enjoy!

These Banana Nut Muffins are a classic and delightful treat. The combination of ripe bananas and nuts creates a moist and flavorful muffin. Perfect for breakfast or as a snack!

Zucchini Bread

Ingredients:

- 2 cups grated zucchini (about 2 medium-sized zucchinis)
- 1 cup granulated sugar
- 1 cup brown sugar, packed
- 1 cup vegetable oil or melted butter
- 3 large eggs
- 2 teaspoons vanilla extract
- 3 cups all-purpose flour
- 1 teaspoon baking powder
- 1/2 teaspoon baking soda
- 1/2 teaspoon salt
- 2 teaspoons ground cinnamon
- 1/2 teaspoon ground nutmeg
- 1/2 cup chopped nuts (walnuts or pecans), optional
- 1/2 cup raisins or chocolate chips, optional

Instructions:

Preheat the Oven:
- Preheat your oven to 350°F (175°C). Grease and flour two 9x5-inch loaf pans.

Grate Zucchini:
- Grate the zucchinis using a grater. If the zucchini has excess moisture, you can squeeze it gently to remove some of the liquid.

Mix Wet Ingredients:

- In a large bowl, combine the grated zucchini, granulated sugar, brown sugar, vegetable oil or melted butter, eggs, and vanilla extract. Mix well.

Combine Dry Ingredients:

- In a separate bowl, whisk together the all-purpose flour, baking powder, baking soda, salt, ground cinnamon, and ground nutmeg.

Combine Wet and Dry Mixtures:

- Add the dry ingredients to the wet ingredients and stir until just combined. Do not overmix.

Add Nuts and Raisins/Chocolate Chips (Optional):

- If using, fold in the chopped nuts and raisins or chocolate chips into the batter.

Fill Loaf Pans:

- Divide the batter evenly between the prepared loaf pans.

Bake:

- Bake in the preheated oven for 55-60 minutes or until a toothpick inserted into the center comes out clean.

Cool:

- Allow the Zucchini Bread to cool in the pans for about 10 minutes, then transfer to a wire rack to cool completely.

Slice and Serve:

- Once cooled, slice the bread and serve. Enjoy!

This Zucchini Bread is moist, flavorful, and a great way to enjoy the abundance of summer zucchinis. It's perfect for breakfast, snacks, or as a sweet treat with a cup of tea or coffee.

Caramelized Onion and Bacon Quiche

Ingredients:

For the Pie Crust:

- 1 1/4 cups all-purpose flour
- 1/2 cup unsalted butter, cold and diced
- 1/4 teaspoon salt
- 3-4 tablespoons ice water

For the Filling:

- 1 tablespoon olive oil
- 2 large onions, thinly sliced
- 6 slices of bacon, cooked and crumbled
- 1 1/2 cups shredded Gruyere or Swiss cheese
- 4 large eggs
- 1 cup heavy cream
- Salt and black pepper to taste
- Fresh thyme leaves for garnish (optional)

Instructions:

For the Pie Crust:

Prepare the Pie Crust:
- In a food processor, combine the flour, cold diced butter, and salt. Pulse until the mixture resembles coarse crumbs.

Add Ice Water:

- With the food processor running, gradually add ice water until the dough starts to come together. Stop the processor and check the dough by squeezing a small amount in your hand. If it holds together, it's ready.

Form a Disk:

- Turn the dough out onto a lightly floured surface and gather it into a ball. Flatten the ball into a disk, wrap it in plastic wrap, and refrigerate for at least 30 minutes.

Roll Out the Dough:

- Preheat your oven to 375°F (190°C). Roll out the chilled dough on a floured surface and fit it into a 9-inch quiche or tart pan. Trim any excess dough.

Pre-Bake the Crust:

- Line the pie crust with parchment paper and fill it with pie weights or dried beans. Bake for about 15 minutes. Remove the weights and parchment, and bake for an additional 5 minutes until the crust is set but not fully cooked. Set aside.

For the Filling:

Caramelize Onions:

- In a skillet, heat olive oil over medium heat. Add thinly sliced onions and cook, stirring occasionally, until caramelized, about 20-25 minutes.

Assemble the Quiche:

- Spread the caramelized onions over the partially baked crust. Sprinkle crumbled bacon over the onions, and then top with shredded Gruyere or Swiss cheese.

Prepare the Egg Mixture:

- In a bowl, whisk together eggs, heavy cream, salt, and black pepper. Pour the egg mixture over the onions, bacon, and cheese in the crust.

Bake the Quiche:

- Bake in the preheated oven for 35-40 minutes or until the center is set and the top is golden brown.

Cool and Garnish:
- Allow the quiche to cool for a few minutes before slicing. Garnish with fresh thyme leaves if desired.

Serve Warm:
- Serve the Caramelized Onion and Bacon Quiche warm. Enjoy!

This quiche is a flavorful and savory dish, perfect for brunch or a special breakfast. The combination of caramelized onions, bacon, and cheese is a classic and delicious choice.

Breakfast BLT

Ingredients:

- 4 slices of your favorite bread (toasted if desired)
- 8 slices of bacon, cooked until crispy
- 1 large tomato, thinly sliced
- 1 cup lettuce leaves (such as iceberg or romaine), washed and patted dry
- Mayonnaise
- Salt and black pepper to taste

Optional Additions:

- Fried or scrambled eggs
- Avocado slices

Instructions:

Cook Bacon:

- Cook the bacon in a skillet over medium heat until it's crispy. Remove excess grease by placing the cooked bacon on a paper towel-lined plate.

Prepare Ingredients:

- Wash and slice the tomato thinly. Wash and pat dry the lettuce leaves.

Toast Bread (Optional):

- Toast the slices of bread if you prefer a toasted BLT.

Spread Mayo:

- Spread a generous layer of mayonnaise on one side of each slice of bread.

Assemble the BLT:

- On the mayo-covered side of one slice of bread, layer half of the bacon slices. Add a layer of tomato slices and lettuce. Season with salt and black pepper to taste.

Optional Additions:

- If desired, add fried or scrambled eggs on top of the lettuce and avocado slices for extra flavor.

Top with Another Slice:

- Place another slice of bread, mayo side down, on top to complete the sandwich.

Repeat for the Second Sandwich:

- Repeat the process to create a second Breakfast BLT sandwich.

Slice and Serve:

- Slice the sandwiches in half diagonally and serve immediately.

Enjoy your Breakfast BLT sandwiches for a delicious and classic breakfast or brunch option! The combination of crispy bacon, fresh tomatoes, and lettuce is always a satisfying choice. Feel free to customize it to your liking with additional ingredients.

Cranberry Orange Muffins

Ingredients:

- 2 cups all-purpose flour
- 1 cup granulated sugar
- 1 tablespoon baking powder
- 1/2 teaspoon baking soda
- 1/4 teaspoon salt
- 1 cup fresh or frozen cranberries, coarsely chopped
- Zest of 1 orange
- 3/4 cup orange juice (freshly squeezed)
- 1/2 cup unsalted butter, melted and cooled
- 2 large eggs
- 1 teaspoon vanilla extract

Optional Glaze:

- 1 cup powdered sugar
- 2 tablespoons orange juice

Instructions:

Preheat the Oven:
- Preheat your oven to 375°F (190°C). Line a muffin tin with paper liners or grease the muffin cups.

Mix Dry Ingredients:
- In a large bowl, whisk together the flour, sugar, baking powder, baking soda, and salt.

Add Cranberries and Orange Zest:

- Gently fold in the chopped cranberries and orange zest into the dry ingredients.

Mix Wet Ingredients:

- In another bowl, whisk together the orange juice, melted butter, eggs, and vanilla extract.

Combine Wet and Dry Mixtures:

- Pour the wet ingredients into the dry ingredients and stir until just combined. Do not overmix; it's okay if there are some lumps.

Fill Muffin Cups:

- Spoon the batter into the muffin cups, filling each about 2/3 full.

Bake:

- Bake in the preheated oven for 18-20 minutes or until a toothpick inserted into the center comes out clean.

Optional Glaze:

- If desired, prepare a simple glaze by whisking together powdered sugar and orange juice. Drizzle the glaze over the cooled muffins.

Cool and Serve:

- Allow the Cranberry Orange Muffins to cool in the muffin tin for a few minutes before transferring them to a wire rack to cool completely.

Enjoy these Cranberry Orange Muffins with a cup of tea or coffee for a delightful treat! The combination of tart cranberries and citrusy orange creates a burst of flavor in every bite.

Nutella Stuffed French Toast

Ingredients:

- 8 slices of your favorite bread (thick slices work well)
- Nutella (as needed for spreading)
- 3 large eggs
- 1/2 cup milk
- 1 teaspoon vanilla extract
- 1/4 teaspoon ground cinnamon
- Pinch of salt
- Butter or cooking spray for greasing the pan
- Powdered sugar for dusting (optional)
- Fresh berries or banana slices for topping (optional)
- Maple syrup for serving

Instructions:

Spread Nutella:
- Take 4 slices of bread and spread a generous layer of Nutella on each slice. Top with the remaining 4 slices of bread to make Nutella sandwiches.

Prepare Egg Mixture:
- In a shallow dish, whisk together the eggs, milk, vanilla extract, ground cinnamon, and a pinch of salt.

Dip the Sandwiches:
- Dip each Nutella sandwich into the egg mixture, ensuring both sides are coated.

Cook on Griddle or Pan:

- Heat a griddle or non-stick pan over medium heat and add a little butter or cooking spray to grease the surface.

Cook French Toast:
- Place the Nutella sandwiches on the griddle or pan and cook until both sides are golden brown and the Nutella is melty. This usually takes 2-3 minutes per side.

Serve:
- Remove the Nutella Stuffed French Toast from the griddle and place them on a serving plate.

Optional Toppings:
- Dust the French toast with powdered sugar and top with fresh berries or banana slices if desired.

Serve Warm with Syrup:
- Serve the Nutella Stuffed French Toast warm with a drizzle of maple syrup.

Enjoy this indulgent and delicious Nutella Stuffed French Toast for a delightful breakfast or brunch treat! The gooey Nutella center adds a sweet and creamy touch to the classic French toast.

Spinach and Mushroom Breakfast Wrap

Ingredients:

- 4 large eggs
- Salt and black pepper to taste
- 1 tablespoon olive oil
- 1 cup sliced mushrooms
- 2 cups fresh spinach leaves, washed
- 4 whole wheat or spinach tortillas
- 1/2 cup shredded cheese (cheddar, feta, or your choice)
- Salsa or hot sauce for serving (optional)
- Avocado slices for garnish (optional)

Instructions:

Scramble Eggs:
- In a bowl, whisk the eggs and season with salt and black pepper to taste.

Sauté Mushrooms and Spinach:
- In a skillet, heat olive oil over medium heat. Add sliced mushrooms and sauté until they release their moisture and become golden brown. Add fresh spinach to the skillet and cook until wilted.

Cook Scrambled Eggs:
- Push the mushrooms and spinach to one side of the skillet and pour the whisked eggs into the other side. Scramble the eggs until cooked through.

Assemble the Wrap:
- Warm the tortillas according to package instructions. Place a portion of the scrambled eggs, sautéed mushrooms, and spinach onto each tortilla.

Add Cheese:

- Sprinkle shredded cheese over the filling while it's still warm, allowing it to melt.

Fold and Roll:

- Fold the sides of the tortilla inwards and then roll it up, creating a wrap.

Optional Garnishes:

- Garnish with avocado slices and drizzle with salsa or hot sauce if desired.

Serve Warm:

- Serve the Spinach and Mushroom Breakfast Wrap warm and enjoy!

This breakfast wrap is not only delicious but also packed with nutrients from the spinach and mushrooms. Feel free to customize it with additional ingredients like diced tomatoes, onions, or your favorite breakfast toppings.

Chocolate Peanut Butter Smoothie

Ingredients:

- 1 banana, frozen
- 1 cup milk (dairy or plant-based)
- 2 tablespoons peanut butter
- 1 tablespoon cocoa powder
- 1 tablespoon honey or maple syrup (optional, for sweetness)
- 1/2 teaspoon vanilla extract
- Ice cubes (optional)

Instructions:

Prepare Ingredients:
- Peel and slice the banana before freezing it. This will add creaminess to the smoothie.

Combine in Blender:
- In a blender, combine the frozen banana slices, milk, peanut butter, cocoa powder, honey or maple syrup (if using), and vanilla extract.

Blend Until Smooth:
- Blend the ingredients until smooth and creamy. If the smoothie is too thick, you can add more milk to reach your desired consistency.

Add Ice Cubes (Optional):
- If you prefer a colder and icier smoothie, you can add a handful of ice cubes and blend again.

Taste and Adjust:

- Taste the smoothie and adjust the sweetness or thickness by adding more honey, cocoa powder, or milk as needed.

Serve Immediately:

- Pour the Chocolate Peanut Butter Smoothie into a glass and serve immediately.

Enjoy this indulgent and satisfying Chocolate Peanut Butter Smoothie as a delicious and energizing treat! It's a perfect option for a quick breakfast or a tasty snack.

Breakfast Nachos

Ingredients:

- 1 tablespoon olive oil
- 1/2 cup diced onion
- 1/2 cup diced bell pepper (any color)
- 1/2 cup cooked and crumbled breakfast sausage or chorizo
- 4 large eggs, scrambled
- Salt and black pepper to taste
- 1 cup shredded cheddar or Mexican blend cheese
- Tortilla chips
- Salsa, guacamole, sour cream, or your favorite toppings for serving

Instructions:

Preheat the Oven:

- Preheat your oven to 375°F (190°C).

Sauté Vegetables:

- In a skillet, heat olive oil over medium heat. Sauté diced onion and bell pepper until softened.

Add Sausage:

- Add the cooked and crumbled breakfast sausage or chorizo to the skillet. Stir to combine with the vegetables.

Scramble Eggs:

- Push the sausage and vegetables to one side of the skillet. Pour the scrambled eggs into the other side. Season with salt and black pepper. Cook the eggs until they are scrambled and cooked through.

Combine Ingredients:
- Mix the scrambled eggs with the sausage and vegetables in the skillet, creating a savory mixture.

Assemble Nachos:
- On a baking sheet or oven-safe dish, arrange a layer of tortilla chips. Spoon the egg and sausage mixture over the chips.

Add Cheese:
- Sprinkle shredded cheddar or Mexican blend cheese over the nachos.

Bake:
- Bake in the preheated oven for about 8-10 minutes or until the cheese is melted and bubbly.

Serve:
- Remove the breakfast nachos from the oven. Top with your favorite toppings such as salsa, guacamole, sour cream, or any other desired additions.

Enjoy:
- Serve the Breakfast Nachos immediately and enjoy this delicious and satisfying breakfast dish!

These Breakfast Nachos are a creative twist on the classic nachos, making them a perfect choice for a savory and hearty breakfast or brunch. Customize with your favorite toppings to suit your taste!

Breakfast Pizza Rolls

Ingredients:

- 1 package (8-ounce) crescent roll dough
- 1/2 cup pizza sauce
- 1 cup shredded mozzarella cheese
- 1/2 cup cooked and crumbled breakfast sausage
- 1/4 cup diced bell pepper
- 1/4 cup diced onion
- 2 large eggs, scrambled
- Salt and black pepper to taste
- Cooking spray

Instructions:

Preheat the Oven:
- Preheat your oven to the temperature specified on the crescent roll dough package.

Prepare Ingredients:
- Cook and crumble the breakfast sausage, scramble the eggs, and dice the bell pepper and onion.

Unroll Crescent Roll Dough:
- On a lightly floured surface, unroll the crescent roll dough into a rectangle.

Spread Pizza Sauce:
- Spread pizza sauce evenly over the crescent roll dough, leaving a small border around the edges.

Add Toppings:

- Sprinkle shredded mozzarella cheese over the sauce. Distribute the cooked breakfast sausage, scrambled eggs, diced bell pepper, and diced onion evenly over the cheese.

Season:
- Season with salt and black pepper to taste.

Roll Up the Dough:
- Starting from one long side, roll up the crescent roll dough with the toppings into a log.

Slice into Rolls:
- Use a sharp knife to slice the rolled dough into 1-inch thick slices, creating pizza rolls.

Place on Baking Sheet:
- Place the pizza rolls on a baking sheet lined with parchment paper and sprayed with cooking spray.

Bake:
- Bake in the preheated oven according to the crescent roll dough package instructions or until the rolls are golden brown and the cheese is melted.

Serve Warm:
- Remove from the oven and let the Breakfast Pizza Rolls cool for a minute before serving.

Enjoy these flavorful and convenient Breakfast Pizza Rolls as a delicious morning treat or for brunch. They are great for a grab-and-go breakfast option!

Breakfast Sushi

Ingredients:

- 2 cups cooked sushi rice, cooled
- 2 tablespoons rice vinegar
- 1 tablespoon sugar
- 1/2 teaspoon salt
- Nori sheets (seaweed sheets)
- Cream cheese, sliced into thin strips
- Smoked salmon, sliced into thin strips
- Avocado, sliced
- Cucumber, julienned
- Scrambled eggs
- Soy sauce for dipping
- Sesame seeds (optional, for garnish)

Instructions:

Prepare Sushi Rice:

- In a small bowl, mix together rice vinegar, sugar, and salt. Add this mixture to the cooked sushi rice and gently fold to combine. Allow the rice to cool to room temperature.

Prepare Ingredients:

- Slice cream cheese, smoked salmon, avocado, and julienned cucumber into thin strips. Prepare scrambled eggs.

Place Nori Sheet:

- Lay a sheet of plastic wrap on a clean surface. Place a nori sheet, shiny side down, on the plastic wrap.

Spread Sushi Rice:
- Wet your hands with water to prevent sticking, then spread a thin layer of sushi rice over the nori, leaving a small border at the top.

Add Ingredients:
- Place strips of cream cheese, smoked salmon, avocado, cucumber, and scrambled eggs horizontally across the rice.

Roll Sushi:
- Starting from the bottom, carefully roll the nori and rice over the ingredients, using the plastic wrap to help you roll. Seal the edge with a little water.

Slice into Rolls:
- Use a sharp knife to slice the rolled sushi into bite-sized pieces.

Repeat:
- Repeat the process with the remaining nori sheets and ingredients.

Serve with Soy Sauce:
- Arrange the Breakfast Sushi on a plate and serve with soy sauce for dipping.

Optional Garnish:
- If desired, sprinkle sesame seeds over the top for garnish.

Enjoy this playful and delicious Breakfast Sushi, where traditional sushi ingredients meet breakfast flavors. It's a unique and visually appealing dish that's perfect for a creative breakfast or brunch!

Pumpkin Spice Pancakes

Ingredients:

- 1 cup all-purpose flour
- 2 tablespoons brown sugar
- 1 teaspoon baking powder
- 1/2 teaspoon baking soda
- 1/2 teaspoon ground cinnamon
- 1/4 teaspoon ground nutmeg
- 1/4 teaspoon ground ginger
- 1/4 teaspoon salt
- 3/4 cup buttermilk
- 1/2 cup pumpkin puree
- 1 large egg
- 2 tablespoons unsalted butter, melted
- 1 teaspoon vanilla extract
- Cooking spray or additional butter for cooking

Optional Toppings:

- Maple syrup
- Whipped cream
- Chopped pecans or walnuts

Instructions:

    Mix Dry Ingredients:

- In a large bowl, whisk together the flour, brown sugar, baking powder, baking soda, ground cinnamon, ground nutmeg, ground ginger, and salt.

Mix Wet Ingredients:

- In another bowl, whisk together the buttermilk, pumpkin puree, egg, melted butter, and vanilla extract.

Combine Wet and Dry Mixtures:

- Pour the wet ingredients into the dry ingredients and stir until just combined. Do not overmix; it's okay if there are some lumps.

Preheat Griddle or Pan:

- Preheat a griddle or non-stick pan over medium heat. Lightly grease with cooking spray or butter.

Cook Pancakes:

- Pour 1/4 cup portions of batter onto the griddle for each pancake. Cook until bubbles form on the surface, then flip and cook until the other side is golden brown.

Repeat:

- Repeat the process until all the batter is used.

Serve Warm:

- Serve the Pumpkin Spice Pancakes warm with your favorite toppings.

Optional Toppings:

- Top with maple syrup, whipped cream, and chopped pecans or walnuts if desired.

Enjoy these Pumpkin Spice Pancakes for a cozy and flavorful breakfast, especially during the fall season!

Maple Pecan Granola

Ingredients:

- 3 cups old-fashioned rolled oats
- 1 cup chopped pecans
- 1/2 cup shredded coconut (optional)
- 1/4 cup chia seeds (optional)
- 1/2 teaspoon ground cinnamon
- 1/4 teaspoon salt
- 1/2 cup maple syrup
- 1/4 cup coconut oil, melted
- 1 teaspoon vanilla extract

Optional Add-Ins:

- 1/2 cup dried cranberries or raisins

Instructions:

Preheat Oven:
- Preheat your oven to 325°F (163°C). Line a baking sheet with parchment paper.

Mix Dry Ingredients:
- In a large bowl, combine the rolled oats, chopped pecans, shredded coconut, chia seeds, ground cinnamon, and salt.

Combine Wet Ingredients:
- In a separate bowl, whisk together the maple syrup, melted coconut oil, and vanilla extract.

Combine Wet and Dry Mixtures:

- Pour the wet ingredients over the dry ingredients and stir until everything is well coated.

Spread on Baking Sheet:

- Spread the granola mixture evenly on the prepared baking sheet.

Bake:

- Bake in the preheated oven for 25-30 minutes or until the granola is golden brown, stirring halfway through to ensure even baking.

Optional Add-Ins:

- If using, add dried cranberries or raisins to the granola after baking and toss to combine.

Cool Completely:

- Allow the granola to cool completely on the baking sheet. It will continue to crisp up as it cools.

Store:

- Once completely cooled, store the Maple Pecan Granola in an airtight container.

Serve:

- Serve with yogurt, milk, or enjoy it as a snack.

This Maple Pecan Granola is not only delicious but also customizable. Feel free to add your favorite dried fruits, seeds, or nuts for a personalized touch!

Biscuits and Gravy

Ingredients:

For the Biscuits:

- 2 cups all-purpose flour
- 1 tablespoon baking powder
- 1 teaspoon sugar
- 1/2 teaspoon salt
- 1/2 cup unsalted butter, cold and cubed
- 3/4 cup milk

For the Sausage Gravy:

- 1 pound ground breakfast sausage
- 1/4 cup all-purpose flour
- 3 cups milk
- Salt and black pepper to taste

Instructions:

For the Biscuits:

Preheat Oven:
- Preheat your oven to 450°F (232°C).

Mix Dry Ingredients:
- In a large bowl, whisk together the flour, baking powder, sugar, and salt.

Cut in Butter:

- Add the cold, cubed butter to the dry ingredients. Use a pastry cutter or your fingers to cut the butter into the flour mixture until it resembles coarse crumbs.

Add Milk:

- Pour in the milk and stir until just combined. Do not overmix.

Knead and Cut:

- Turn the dough out onto a floured surface and knead it gently a few times. Pat the dough to about 1/2-inch thickness. Use a biscuit cutter to cut out biscuits.

Bake:

- Place the biscuits on a baking sheet and bake for 10-12 minutes or until golden brown.

For the Sausage Gravy:

Cook Sausage:

- In a skillet over medium heat, cook the ground breakfast sausage, breaking it into crumbles as it cooks. Cook until browned and cooked through.

Make Roux:

- Sprinkle flour over the cooked sausage and stir to combine, creating a roux.

Add Milk:

- Gradually pour in the milk while stirring constantly to avoid lumps. Continue cooking and stirring until the mixture thickens.

Season:

- Season the gravy with salt and black pepper to taste. Adjust the seasoning as needed.

Serve:

- Split the biscuits in half and spoon the sausage gravy over the top.

Enjoy this hearty and comforting Biscuits and Gravy dish for a classic breakfast or brunch option!

Dutch Baby Pancake

Ingredients:

- 3 large eggs
- 2/3 cup all-purpose flour
- 2/3 cup milk
- 1 tablespoon granulated sugar
- 1/2 teaspoon vanilla extract
- 1/4 teaspoon salt
- 3 tablespoons unsalted butter
- Powdered sugar, for dusting
- Fresh berries or maple syrup for serving (optional)

Instructions:

Preheat Oven:

- Preheat your oven to 425°F (220°C).

Blend Batter:

- In a blender, combine the eggs, flour, milk, sugar, vanilla extract, and salt. Blend until the batter is smooth.

Heat Butter in Pan:

- In an oven-safe skillet (10-12 inches in diameter), melt the butter over medium heat on the stovetop.

Pour Batter:

- Once the butter is melted and bubbling, pour the batter into the skillet.

Bake:

- Transfer the skillet to the preheated oven and bake for 18-20 minutes or until the Dutch Baby Pancake is puffed up and golden brown around the edges.

Serve:

- Carefully remove the skillet from the oven. The Dutch Baby Pancake will deflate slightly. Dust it with powdered sugar and serve immediately.

Optional Toppings:

- Serve with fresh berries, a drizzle of maple syrup, or your favorite pancake toppings.

The Dutch Baby Pancake is a delightful and impressive pancake that's easy to make. It's perfect for breakfast or brunch, and its dramatic rise in the oven makes it a fun dish to serve!

Breakfast Fajitas

Ingredients:

For Fajita Filling:

- 1 tablespoon vegetable oil
- 1 bell pepper, thinly sliced
- 1 onion, thinly sliced
- 1 cup cooked and sliced breakfast sausage or chorizo
- Salt and black pepper to taste
- 4 large eggs, scrambled

For Serving:

- Flour tortillas
- Shredded cheese
- Salsa
- Guacamole
- Sour cream
- Chopped cilantro
- Lime wedges

Instructions:

Prepare Fajita Filling:
- In a large skillet, heat vegetable oil over medium heat. Add sliced bell pepper and onion. Cook until they are softened and slightly caramelized.

Add Sausage or Chorizo:

- Add the cooked and sliced breakfast sausage or chorizo to the skillet. Stir to combine with the peppers and onions.

Season:
- Season the mixture with salt and black pepper to taste. Continue cooking until everything is heated through.

Scramble Eggs:
- Push the sausage, pepper, and onion mixture to one side of the skillet. Pour the scrambled eggs into the other side. Scramble the eggs until they are cooked through.

Combine Ingredients:
- Mix the scrambled eggs with the sausage, peppers, and onions in the skillet, creating a flavorful fajita filling.

Warm Tortillas:
- Warm the flour tortillas in a dry skillet or microwave according to package instructions.

Assemble Breakfast Fajitas:
- Spoon the fajita filling onto the warm tortillas.

Add Toppings:
- Top the fajitas with shredded cheese, salsa, guacamole, sour cream, and chopped cilantro.

Serve with Lime Wedges:
- Serve the Breakfast Fajitas with lime wedges on the side for squeezing over the top.

Enjoy these Breakfast Fajitas for a flavorful and satisfying morning meal! Customize them with your favorite toppings and serve them with a side of fresh fruit or potatoes if desired.

Ham and Cheese Croissant

Ingredients:

- 4 large croissants
- 8 slices of ham
- 4 slices of Swiss cheese (or your favorite cheese)
- Dijon mustard (optional)
- 2 tablespoons unsalted butter, melted
- 1 tablespoon honey (optional, for a sweet touch)
- Sesame seeds or poppy seeds for sprinkling (optional)

Instructions:

Preheat Oven:
- Preheat your oven to 350°F (180°C).

Slice Croissants:
- Carefully slice each croissant horizontally, creating a top and bottom half.

Assemble Croissants:
- Place a slice of ham on the bottom half of each croissant. Add a slice of Swiss cheese on top of the ham. If desired, spread a thin layer of Dijon mustard on the top half of the croissant.

Close Croissants:
- Place the top half of the croissants over the ham and cheese to close the sandwiches.

Brush with Butter and Honey:
- In a small bowl, mix melted butter and honey. Brush the tops of the croissants with this mixture.

Optional Seeds:

- If using sesame seeds or poppy seeds, sprinkle them over the buttered tops.

Bake:

- Place the assembled croissants on a baking sheet and bake in the preheated oven for about 10 minutes or until the cheese is melted, and the croissants are heated through.

Serve Warm:

- Remove from the oven and serve the Ham and Cheese Croissants warm.

These Ham and Cheese Croissants are a delightful combination of flaky croissants, savory ham, and melted cheese. They make for a delicious breakfast or brunch option. Enjoy!

Breakfast Polenta with Poached Egg

Ingredients:

For the Polenta:

- 1 cup polenta or cornmeal
- 4 cups water
- 1 teaspoon salt
- 1/2 cup grated Parmesan cheese (optional)
- 2 tablespoons unsalted butter (optional)

For Poached Eggs:

- 4 large eggs
- 1 tablespoon white vinegar (for poaching water)
- Salt and black pepper to taste

Optional Toppings:

- Fresh herbs (e.g., chopped chives or parsley)
- Red pepper flakes
- Grated Parmesan cheese

Instructions:

For the Polenta:

Cook Polenta:
- In a medium saucepan, bring 4 cups of water to a boil. Add salt and slowly whisk in the polenta or cornmeal, stirring continuously to avoid lumps.

Reduce Heat and Simmer:

- Reduce the heat to low and let the polenta simmer, stirring frequently, until it thickens and becomes creamy. This usually takes about 15-20 minutes.

Optional Add-Ins:

- If desired, stir in grated Parmesan cheese and butter to add extra flavor and creaminess.

Keep Warm:

- Once the polenta reaches the desired consistency, cover the saucepan and keep it warm on low heat while preparing the poached eggs.

For Poached Eggs:

Poach Eggs:

- Bring a medium-sized pot of water to a simmer. Add 1 tablespoon of white vinegar to the simmering water.

Crack Eggs:

- Crack each egg into a small bowl or cup.

Create a Whirlpool:

- Create a gentle whirlpool in the simmering water using a spoon. Carefully slide the egg into the center of the whirlpool.

Poach Eggs:

- Allow the eggs to poach for about 3-4 minutes for a runny yolk or longer if you prefer a firmer yolk.

Remove with Slotted Spoon:

- Use a slotted spoon to carefully lift each poached egg out of the water, allowing excess water to drain.

Assemble Breakfast Polenta with Poached Egg

Serve:

- Spoon a generous portion of warm polenta onto a plate. Place a poached egg on top.

Season and Garnish:

- Season with salt and black pepper. Garnish with fresh herbs, red pepper flakes, and additional grated Parmesan cheese if desired.

Serve Warm:

- Serve the Breakfast Polenta with Poached Egg immediately while warm.

Enjoy this comforting and savory Breakfast Polenta with Poached Egg for a hearty and satisfying morning meal!

Lemon Poppy Seed Pancakes

Ingredients:

- 1 cup all-purpose flour
- 2 tablespoons granulated sugar
- 1 teaspoon baking powder
- 1/2 teaspoon baking soda
- 1/4 teaspoon salt
- 1 cup buttermilk
- 1 large egg
- 2 tablespoons unsalted butter, melted
- Zest of 1 lemon
- 1 tablespoon fresh lemon juice
- 1 tablespoon poppy seeds
- Cooking spray or additional butter for cooking

Optional Toppings:

- Maple syrup
- Fresh berries
- Powdered sugar

Instructions:

Mix Dry Ingredients:
- In a large bowl, whisk together the flour, sugar, baking powder, baking soda, and salt.

Mix Wet Ingredients:

- In a separate bowl, whisk together the buttermilk, egg, melted butter, lemon zest, lemon juice, and poppy seeds.

Combine Wet and Dry Mixtures:

- Pour the wet ingredients into the dry ingredients and stir until just combined. Do not overmix; it's okay if there are some lumps.

Preheat Griddle or Pan:

- Preheat a griddle or non-stick pan over medium heat. Lightly grease with cooking spray or butter.

Cook Pancakes:

- Pour 1/4 cup portions of batter onto the griddle for each pancake. Cook until bubbles form on the surface, then flip and cook until the other side is golden brown.

Repeat:

- Repeat the process until all the batter is used.

Serve Warm:

- Serve the Lemon Poppy Seed Pancakes warm with your favorite toppings.

Optional Toppings:

- Top with maple syrup, fresh berries, and a dusting of powdered sugar if desired.

Enjoy these light and flavorful Lemon Poppy Seed Pancakes for a bright and delicious breakfast or brunch!

Blueberry Banana Bread

Ingredients:

- 2 to 3 ripe bananas, mashed
- 1/2 cup unsalted butter, melted
- 1 teaspoon vanilla extract
- 1 cup granulated sugar
- 1 large egg
- 1 1/2 cups all-purpose flour
- 1 teaspoon baking soda
- 1/2 teaspoon baking powder
- 1/2 teaspoon salt
- 1 cup fresh or frozen blueberries (if using frozen, do not thaw)

Optional Add-ins:

- 1/2 cup chopped nuts (e.g., walnuts or pecans)
- 1/2 teaspoon cinnamon

Instructions:

Preheat Oven:
- Preheat your oven to 350°F (175°C). Grease a 9x5-inch loaf pan.

Mash Bananas:
- In a large bowl, mash the ripe bananas with a fork or potato masher.

Add Wet Ingredients:
- Add melted butter, vanilla extract, sugar, and the egg to the mashed bananas. Stir until well combined.

Combine Dry Ingredients:

- In a separate bowl, whisk together the flour, baking soda, baking powder, and salt.

Mix Wet and Dry Ingredients:

- Add the dry ingredients to the banana mixture and stir until just combined. Do not overmix.

Add Blueberries (and Nuts):

- Gently fold in the blueberries. If using nuts, fold them in as well.

Pour into Pan:

- Pour the batter into the prepared loaf pan.

Bake:

- Bake in the preheated oven for 60-70 minutes or until a toothpick inserted into the center comes out clean.

Cool:

- Allow the Blueberry Banana Bread to cool in the pan for about 10 minutes, then transfer it to a wire rack to cool completely.

Slice and Serve:

- Once cooled, slice and serve. Enjoy your delicious Blueberry Banana Bread!

This recipe yields a moist and flavorful banana bread with bursts of juicy blueberries. Feel free to customize it by adding nuts or a hint of cinnamon for extra flavor.

Breakfast Bruschetta

Ingredients:

- Baguette or crusty bread, sliced
- Olive oil for brushing
- 4 large eggs
- Salt and black pepper to taste
- 1 cup cherry tomatoes, diced
- 1/2 cup fresh mozzarella, diced
- Fresh basil leaves, chopped
- Balsamic glaze for drizzling (optional)

Instructions:

Preheat Oven:
- Preheat your oven to broil.

Prepare Bread:
- Place the sliced baguette or crusty bread on a baking sheet. Brush each slice with olive oil.

Toast Bread:
- Toast the bread slices under the broiler for 1-2 minutes or until they are golden brown. Keep an eye on them to prevent burning.

Cook Eggs:
- While the bread is toasting, cook the eggs. You can prepare them as fried eggs or scrambled eggs, depending on your preference. Season with salt and black pepper.

Assemble Bruschetta:

- In a bowl, combine diced cherry tomatoes, fresh mozzarella, and chopped basil. Mix well.

Top Toasted Bread:

- Place a spoonful of the tomato and mozzarella mixture on each toasted bread slice.

Add Eggs:

- Top each bruschetta with a cooked egg.

Season:

- Sprinkle with additional salt and black pepper to taste.

Optional Drizzle:

- Drizzle balsamic glaze over the top for added flavor (optional).

Serve:

- Serve the Breakfast Bruschetta immediately while the bread is still warm and the eggs are cooked to your liking.

Enjoy this Breakfast Bruschetta as a delicious and savory morning treat with a perfect combination of flavors!

Cheesy Grits

Ingredients:

- 1 cup grits (not instant)
- 4 cups water
- 1 teaspoon salt
- 1 cup shredded cheddar cheese
- 1/4 cup unsalted butter
- 1/2 cup milk
- Salt and black pepper to taste

Optional Toppings:

- Additional shredded cheese
- Chopped green onions or chives
- Crumbled bacon

Instructions:

Cook Grits:

- In a medium-sized saucepan, bring 4 cups of water to a boil. Stir in the grits and 1 teaspoon of salt.

Reduce Heat and Simmer:

- Reduce the heat to low, cover the saucepan, and let the grits simmer, stirring occasionally, until they are thick and creamy. This usually takes about 20-25 minutes.

Add Cheese and Butter:

- Once the grits are cooked, stir in the shredded cheddar cheese and unsalted butter. Continue stirring until the cheese and butter are melted and well incorporated into the grits.

Add Milk:

- Pour in the milk and stir until the grits reach your desired creamy consistency. If needed, you can add more milk.

Season:

- Season the cheesy grits with salt and black pepper to taste. Adjust the seasoning as needed.

Serve Warm:

- Serve the Cheesy Grits warm.

Optional Toppings:

- If desired, top the cheesy grits with additional shredded cheese, chopped green onions or chives, and crumbled bacon.

Enjoy these creamy and flavorful Cheesy Grits as a comforting side dish for breakfast or as a delicious accompaniment to a variety of main courses!

Breakfast Empanadas

Ingredients:

For the Dough:

- 2 1/2 cups all-purpose flour
- 1/2 teaspoon salt
- 1 cup unsalted butter, cold and diced
- 1/2 cup cold water

For the Filling:

- 1 tablespoon olive oil
- 1/2 cup onion, finely chopped
- 1/2 cup bell pepper, finely chopped
- 1/2 cup cooked breakfast sausage or chorizo
- 4 large eggs, scrambled
- Salt and black pepper to taste
- 1 cup shredded cheddar cheese
- Optional: salsa or hot sauce for serving

Instructions:

For the Dough:

    Mix Flour and Salt:
- In a large bowl, whisk together the flour and salt.

    Add Butter:

- Add the diced cold butter to the flour mixture. Use your fingers or a pastry cutter to cut the butter into the flour until the mixture resembles coarse crumbs.

Add Water:

- Gradually add cold water, mixing until the dough comes together. Form the dough into a ball, wrap it in plastic wrap, and refrigerate for at least 30 minutes.

For the Filling:

Cook Vegetables:

- In a skillet, heat olive oil over medium heat. Add chopped onion and bell pepper. Cook until softened.

Add Sausage and Eggs:

- Add cooked breakfast sausage or chorizo to the skillet. Stir in scrambled eggs and cook until the eggs are just set.

Season and Add Cheese:

- Season the filling with salt and black pepper to taste. Stir in shredded cheddar cheese until melted. Remove from heat.

Assemble and Bake:

Preheat Oven:

- Preheat your oven to 375°F (190°C).

Roll Out Dough:

- On a floured surface, roll out the chilled dough to about 1/8-inch thickness.

Cut Dough Circles:

- Use a round cutter or a glass to cut out circles from the rolled-out dough.

Add Filling:

- Place a spoonful of the breakfast filling in the center of each dough circle.

Fold and Seal:

- Fold the dough over the filling to create a half-moon shape. Press the edges to seal, and use a fork to crimp the edges.

Bake:

- Place the assembled empanadas on a baking sheet and bake in the preheated oven for 15-20 minutes or until golden brown.

Serve:

- Allow the Breakfast Empanadas to cool slightly before serving. Optionally, serve with salsa or hot sauce.

These Breakfast Empanadas are a delicious and portable morning meal. Enjoy them for breakfast or brunch with your favorite dipping sauce!

Caprese Avocado Toast

Ingredients:

- 2 slices of your favorite bread (sourdough or whole grain work well)
- 1 ripe avocado
- 1 medium-sized tomato, sliced
- Fresh mozzarella cheese, sliced
- Fresh basil leaves
- Balsamic glaze (optional)
- Salt and black pepper to taste
- Olive oil for drizzling (optional)

Instructions:

Toast Bread:
- Toast the slices of bread to your desired level of crispiness.

Prepare Avocado:
- While the bread is toasting, mash the ripe avocado in a bowl using a fork. Add salt and black pepper to taste.

Assemble Avocado Toast:
- Spread the mashed avocado evenly onto each slice of toasted bread.

Layer Tomatoes:
- Place tomato slices on top of the mashed avocado.

Add Mozzarella and Basil:
- Add slices of fresh mozzarella cheese on top of the tomatoes. Place fresh basil leaves on top for added flavor.

Drizzle and Season:

- Drizzle with balsamic glaze if desired. You can also add a touch of olive oil for extra richness. Season with additional salt and black pepper to taste.

Serve:
- Serve the Caprese Avocado Toast immediately while the bread is still warm.

Enjoy this refreshing and flavorful Caprese Avocado Toast for a delightful breakfast or light lunch!

Mango Coconut Chia Pudding

Ingredients:

- 1/4 cup chia seeds
- 1 cup coconut milk (full-fat for creamier pudding)
- 1 ripe mango, peeled and diced
- 1 tablespoon honey or maple syrup (optional, depending on your sweetness preference)
- 1/2 teaspoon vanilla extract
- Shredded coconut and additional mango slices for garnish (optional)

Instructions:

Prepare Chia Seed Mixture:

- In a bowl, combine chia seeds and coconut milk. Stir well to ensure that the chia seeds are evenly distributed in the liquid.

Sweeten and Flavor:

- Add honey or maple syrup (if using) and vanilla extract to the chia seed mixture. Mix thoroughly.

Chill:

- Cover the bowl and refrigerate the chia seed mixture for at least 4 hours or overnight. This allows the chia seeds to absorb the liquid and create a pudding-like consistency.

Prepare Mango:

- In the meantime, peel and dice the ripe mango.

Assemble Chia Pudding:

- Once the chia pudding has set, give it a good stir. Spoon a portion of the chia pudding into serving glasses or bowls.

Layer with Mango:

- Add a layer of diced mango on top of the chia pudding.

Repeat Layers:

- Repeat the layers until you fill the serving glasses or bowls, finishing with a layer of diced mango on top.

Garnish (Optional):

- Garnish with shredded coconut and additional mango slices if desired.

Serve:

- Serve the Mango Coconut Chia Pudding chilled.

This Mango Coconut Chia Pudding is not only delicious but also packed with healthy nutrients. It makes for a delightful breakfast or a satisfying dessert. Enjoy!

Breakfast Tostadas

Ingredients:

- 4 corn tostada shells
- 4 large eggs
- 1 tablespoon olive oil
- 1 cup black beans, cooked and drained
- 1 cup cherry tomatoes, halved
- 1 avocado, sliced
- 1/2 cup shredded cheddar or Mexican blend cheese
- Fresh cilantro, chopped (for garnish)
- Salt and black pepper to taste
- Hot sauce or salsa (optional, for serving)

Instructions:

Cook Eggs:
- In a skillet, heat olive oil over medium heat. Crack the eggs into the skillet and cook them to your desired doneness. Season with salt and black pepper.

Warm Black Beans:
- In a separate pan, heat the black beans until warmed through.

Assemble Tostadas:
- Place a tostada shell on each serving plate.

Layer Ingredients:
- Spread a layer of black beans on each tostada shell. Top with a cooked egg.

Add Tomatoes and Avocado:
- Arrange halved cherry tomatoes and sliced avocado on top of the eggs.

Sprinkle Cheese:

- Sprinkle shredded cheese over the ingredients on each tostada.

Garnish:

- Garnish with chopped cilantro for added freshness.

Serve:

- Serve the Breakfast Tostadas immediately while the eggs are warm.

Optional:

- Drizzle with hot sauce or serve with salsa on the side if you like a bit of heat.

Enjoy these Breakfast Tostadas for a flavorful and satisfying morning meal! Feel free to customize the toppings based on your preferences.

Breakfast Slaw

Ingredients:

For the Slaw:

- 2 cups shredded cabbage (green or red)
- 1 cup shredded carrots
- 1 cup jicama, julienned
- 1/2 cup red bell pepper, thinly sliced
- 1/4 cup red onion, thinly sliced
- 1/4 cup fresh cilantro, chopped

For the Dressing:

- 2 tablespoons Greek yogurt
- 1 tablespoon mayonnaise
- 1 tablespoon apple cider vinegar
- 1 tablespoon honey
- Salt and black pepper to taste

Optional Toppings:

- Poached or fried eggs
- Avocado slices
- Toasted nuts or seeds (e.g., sunflower seeds or sliced almonds)

Instructions:

Prepare Vegetables:

- In a large bowl, combine shredded cabbage, shredded carrots, julienned jicama, sliced red bell pepper, sliced red onion, and chopped cilantro.

Make Dressing:

- In a small bowl, whisk together Greek yogurt, mayonnaise, apple cider vinegar, honey, salt, and black pepper. Adjust the seasoning to taste.

Toss and Coat:

- Pour the dressing over the slaw ingredients. Toss the slaw until the vegetables are evenly coated with the dressing.

Chill:

- Cover the bowl and refrigerate the breakfast slaw for at least 30 minutes to allow the flavors to meld.

Serve:

- When ready to serve, portion the breakfast slaw onto plates or bowls.

Optional Toppings:

- Top each serving with a poached or fried egg, avocado slices, and toasted nuts or seeds if desired.

Enjoy:

- Enjoy the refreshing and crunchy Breakfast Slaw as a nutritious and vibrant start to your day!

This breakfast slaw is not only delicious but also a great way to incorporate a variety of vegetables into your morning routine. Feel free to customize the ingredients based on your preferences.

Bacon and Spinach Breakfast Wrap

Ingredients:

- 4 large flour tortillas
- 8 slices of bacon
- 4 large eggs
- 1 cup baby spinach leaves
- 1/2 cup shredded cheddar cheese
- Salt and black pepper to taste
- Hot sauce or salsa (optional, for serving)

Instructions:

Cook Bacon:
- In a skillet over medium heat, cook the bacon until crispy. Remove from the skillet and drain on paper towels. Set aside.

Cook Eggs:
- In the same skillet, remove some of the excess bacon grease, leaving about a tablespoon in the pan. Crack the eggs into the skillet and cook to your desired doneness. Season with salt and black pepper.

Assemble Wraps:
- Warm the flour tortillas. Place a tortilla on a flat surface.

Add Spinach and Eggs:
- Place a handful of baby spinach leaves in the center of each tortilla. Top with a portion of the cooked eggs.

Layer with Bacon and Cheese:

- Add 2 slices of crispy bacon on top of the eggs. Sprinkle shredded cheddar cheese over the bacon.

Fold and Roll:

- Fold the sides of the tortilla over the filling, then roll it tightly into a wrap.

Serve:

- Serve the Bacon and Spinach Breakfast Wraps immediately.

Optional:

- Serve with hot sauce or salsa on the side for added flavor.

Enjoy these hearty and flavorful Bacon and Spinach Breakfast Wraps for a satisfying breakfast on the go!

Oat Bran Muffins

Ingredients:

- 1 cup oat bran
- 1/2 cup whole wheat flour
- 1/2 cup all-purpose flour
- 1/2 cup brown sugar, packed
- 1 teaspoon baking powder
- 1/2 teaspoon baking soda
- 1/2 teaspoon salt
- 1 teaspoon ground cinnamon
- 1 cup buttermilk
- 1/4 cup vegetable oil
- 1 large egg
- 1 teaspoon vanilla extract
- 1/2 cup raisins or chopped nuts (optional)

Instructions:

Preheat Oven:
- Preheat your oven to 375°F (190°C). Line a muffin tin with paper liners or grease the muffin cups.

Mix Dry Ingredients:
- In a large bowl, whisk together oat bran, whole wheat flour, all-purpose flour, brown sugar, baking powder, baking soda, salt, and ground cinnamon.

Combine Wet Ingredients:

- In a separate bowl, whisk together buttermilk, vegetable oil, egg, and vanilla extract.

Combine Mixtures:

- Pour the wet ingredients into the dry ingredients. Stir until just combined. Do not overmix. If using, fold in raisins or chopped nuts.

Fill Muffin Cups:

- Spoon the batter into the prepared muffin cups, filling each about 2/3 full.

Bake:

- Bake in the preheated oven for 15-18 minutes or until a toothpick inserted into the center of a muffin comes out clean.

Cool:

- Allow the muffins to cool in the tin for a few minutes, then transfer them to a wire rack to cool completely.

Serve:

- Serve the Oat Bran Muffins and enjoy!

These Oat Bran Muffins are a wholesome and delicious choice for breakfast or a snack. Feel free to customize them with your favorite additions like fruits or nuts.

Pesto and Tomato Breakfast Sandwich

Ingredients:

- 2 English muffins, split and toasted
- 4 large eggs
- 4 slices of ripe tomato
- 4 tablespoons pesto sauce
- 4 slices of mozzarella or your favorite cheese
- Salt and black pepper to taste
- Olive oil or butter for cooking

Instructions:

Cook Eggs:

- In a skillet over medium heat, add a little olive oil or butter. Crack the eggs into the skillet and cook to your desired doneness. Season with salt and black pepper.

Assemble Sandwiches:

- Spread a tablespoon of pesto sauce on each half of the toasted English muffins.

Add Tomato Slices:

- Place a slice of ripe tomato on the bottom half of each English muffin.

Top with Eggs and Cheese:

- Place a cooked egg on top of the tomato. Add a slice of mozzarella or your favorite cheese.

Cover and Melt Cheese:

- Top each sandwich with the other half of the toasted English muffin to create a sandwich. Allow the residual heat to melt the cheese slightly.

Serve:

- Serve the Pesto and Tomato Breakfast Sandwiches immediately.

Enjoy these flavorful and satisfying breakfast sandwiches with the combination of pesto, ripe tomatoes, and melted cheese!

Sausage Gravy Biscuits

Ingredients:

For the Biscuits:

- 2 cups all-purpose flour
- 1 tablespoon baking powder
- 1 teaspoon sugar
- 1/2 teaspoon salt
- 1/2 cup unsalted butter, cold and diced
- 3/4 cup buttermilk

For the Sausage Gravy:

- 1 lb breakfast sausage (pork or turkey)
- 1/4 cup all-purpose flour
- 3 cups milk
- Salt and black pepper to taste

Instructions:

For the Biscuits:

Preheat Oven:
- Preheat your oven to 425°F (220°C).

Mix Dry Ingredients:
- In a large bowl, whisk together the flour, baking powder, sugar, and salt.

Add Butter:

- Add the cold, diced butter to the dry ingredients. Use a pastry cutter or your fingers to cut the butter into the flour until it resembles coarse crumbs.

Add Buttermilk:

- Pour in the buttermilk and stir until just combined. Do not overmix.

Form Dough:

- Turn the dough out onto a floured surface. Pat it into a rectangle and fold it over onto itself. Repeat this process a few times to create layers.

Cut Biscuits:

- Roll the dough to about 1/2-inch thickness. Use a biscuit cutter to cut out biscuits and place them on a baking sheet.

Bake:

- Bake in the preheated oven for 12-15 minutes or until the biscuits are golden brown.

For the Sausage Gravy:

Cook Sausage:

- In a large skillet over medium heat, cook the breakfast sausage, breaking it apart with a spoon, until browned and cooked through.

Make Roux:

- Sprinkle the cooked sausage with flour and stir to coat. Cook for a couple of minutes to remove the raw flour taste.

Add Milk:

- Gradually whisk in the milk, stirring constantly to avoid lumps. Bring the mixture to a simmer.

Season:

- Season the sausage gravy with salt and black pepper to taste. Continue to simmer until the gravy thickens to your desired consistency.

Serve:

- Serve the sausage gravy over the warm biscuits.

Enjoy these comforting Sausage Gravy and Biscuits for a hearty and satisfying breakfast!

Ricotta Pancakes

Ingredients:

- 1 cup all-purpose flour
- 1 tablespoon sugar
- 1 teaspoon baking powder
- 1/2 teaspoon baking soda
- 1/4 teaspoon salt
- 3/4 cup ricotta cheese
- 3/4 cup milk
- 2 large eggs
- 1 teaspoon vanilla extract
- Zest of 1 lemon (optional)
- Butter or oil for cooking

Optional Toppings:

- Fresh berries
- Maple syrup
- Powdered sugar

Instructions:

    Mix Dry Ingredients:
- In a large bowl, whisk together the flour, sugar, baking powder, baking soda, and salt.

    Combine Wet Ingredients:

- In a separate bowl, whisk together ricotta cheese, milk, eggs, vanilla extract, and lemon zest (if using).

Combine Mixtures:

- Pour the wet ingredients into the dry ingredients. Stir until just combined. The batter may be a bit lumpy; avoid overmixing.

Preheat Griddle or Pan:

- Preheat a griddle or non-stick pan over medium heat. Add a little butter or oil to grease the surface.

Cook Pancakes:

- Pour 1/4 cup portions of batter onto the griddle for each pancake. Cook until bubbles form on the surface, then flip and cook until the other side is golden brown.

Repeat:

- Repeat the process until all the batter is used.

Serve Warm:

- Serve the Ricotta Pancakes warm with your favorite toppings.

Optional Toppings:

- Top with fresh berries, drizzle with maple syrup, and dust with powdered sugar if desired.

Enjoy these light and fluffy Ricotta Pancakes for a delightful breakfast or brunch!

Blackberry Lemon Scones

Ingredients:

- 2 cups all-purpose flour
- 1/4 cup granulated sugar
- 1 tablespoon baking powder
- 1/2 teaspoon salt
- Zest of 1 lemon
- 1/2 cup unsalted butter, cold and diced
- 1/2 cup milk
- 1 large egg
- 1 teaspoon vanilla extract
- 1 cup fresh blackberries

For the Glaze:

- 1 cup powdered sugar
- 2 tablespoons fresh lemon juice
- Zest of 1 lemon

Instructions:

Preheat Oven:
- Preheat your oven to 400°F (200°C). Line a baking sheet with parchment paper.

Mix Dry Ingredients:
- In a large bowl, whisk together the flour, sugar, baking powder, salt, and lemon zest.

Add Butter:

- Add the cold, diced butter to the dry ingredients. Use a pastry cutter or your fingers to cut the butter into the flour until it resembles coarse crumbs.

Combine Wet Ingredients:

- In a separate bowl, whisk together the milk, egg, and vanilla extract.

Combine Mixtures:

- Pour the wet ingredients into the dry ingredients. Stir until just combined. Do not overmix.

Add Blackberries:

- Gently fold in the fresh blackberries.

Shape Dough:

- Turn the dough out onto a floured surface. Pat it into a circle about 1-inch thick.

Cut Scones:

- Use a sharp knife or a biscuit cutter to cut the dough into scones.

Bake:

- Place the scones on the prepared baking sheet and bake for 15-18 minutes or until they are golden brown.

Make Glaze:

- While the scones are baking, prepare the glaze by whisking together powdered sugar, fresh lemon juice, and lemon zest.

Glaze Scones:

- Once the scones are cooled slightly, drizzle the lemon glaze over the top.

Serve:

- Serve the Blackberry Lemon Scones and enjoy!

These scones are a delightful combination of tart blackberries and zesty lemon. Perfect for a morning treat or afternoon tea!

Breakfast Pita Pockets

Ingredients:

- 4 whole wheat pita pockets
- 4 large eggs
- 1 cup cherry tomatoes, halved
- 1/2 cucumber, diced
- 1/4 cup red onion, finely chopped
- 1/2 cup feta cheese, crumbled
- Fresh parsley, chopped (for garnish)
- Salt and black pepper to taste
- Olive oil for cooking

Optional Toppings:

- Greek yogurt or tzatziki sauce

Instructions:

Preheat Oven:

- Preheat your oven to 350°F (175°C).

Warm Pitas:

- Place the pita pockets in the oven to warm them for a few minutes.

Cook Eggs:

- In a skillet, heat olive oil over medium heat. Crack the eggs into the skillet and cook to your desired doneness. Season with salt and black pepper.

Prepare Vegetables:

- In a bowl, combine cherry tomatoes, diced cucumber, and finely chopped red onion.

Assemble Pita Pockets:

- Take the warmed pita pockets and carefully open them to create a pocket. Stuff each pocket with a cooked egg and a portion of the vegetable mixture.

Add Feta Cheese:

- Sprinkle crumbled feta cheese over the eggs and vegetables in each pita pocket.

Garnish:

- Garnish with fresh parsley for added freshness.

Optional Toppings:

- Drizzle with Greek yogurt or tzatziki sauce if desired.

Serve:

- Serve the Breakfast Pita Pockets warm.

Enjoy these wholesome and customizable Breakfast Pita Pockets for a delicious and filling morning meal!

Breakfast Stuffed Mushrooms

Ingredients:

- 8 large mushrooms, cleaned and stems removed
- 1/2 pound breakfast sausage (pork or turkey)
- 1/4 cup onion, finely chopped
- 1/4 cup bell pepper, finely chopped
- 1/4 cup cherry tomatoes, diced
- 4 large eggs
- Salt and black pepper to taste
- 1/2 cup shredded cheddar cheese
- Fresh parsley, chopped (for garnish)

Instructions:

Preheat Oven:
- Preheat your oven to 375°F (190°C).

Prepare Mushrooms:
- Remove the stems from the mushrooms and clean the caps. Place the mushroom caps on a baking sheet.

Cook Sausage:
- In a skillet over medium heat, cook the breakfast sausage, breaking it apart with a spoon, until browned and cooked through.

Add Vegetables:
- Add finely chopped onion, bell pepper, and diced cherry tomatoes to the skillet with the sausage. Cook until the vegetables are softened.

Prepare Eggs:

- Push the sausage and vegetable mixture to the side of the skillet. Crack the eggs into the skillet and scramble them. Mix the scrambled eggs with the sausage and vegetables.

Season:

- Season the mixture with salt and black pepper to taste. Stir until everything is well combined.

Fill Mushrooms:

- Spoon the sausage, vegetable, and egg mixture into each mushroom cap, pressing down gently to pack the filling.

Top with Cheese:

- Sprinkle shredded cheddar cheese over the top of each stuffed mushroom.

Bake:

- Bake in the preheated oven for 15-20 minutes or until the mushrooms are tender and the cheese is melted and bubbly.

Garnish:

- Garnish the Breakfast Stuffed Mushrooms with chopped fresh parsley.

Serve:

- Serve the stuffed mushrooms warm.

Enjoy these flavorful and protein-packed Breakfast Stuffed Mushrooms for a delicious and satisfying breakfast!

Sweet Potato Pancakes

Ingredients:

- 1 cup mashed sweet potatoes (cooked and cooled)
- 1 cup all-purpose flour
- 1 tablespoon brown sugar
- 1 teaspoon baking powder
- 1/2 teaspoon baking soda
- 1/2 teaspoon ground cinnamon
- 1/4 teaspoon ground nutmeg
- 1/4 teaspoon salt
- 1 cup buttermilk
- 1 large egg
- 2 tablespoons unsalted butter, melted
- 1 teaspoon vanilla extract
- Maple syrup and chopped nuts for serving (optional)

Instructions:

Prepare Sweet Potatoes:
- Cook sweet potatoes until tender. Mash and let them cool.

Mix Dry Ingredients:
- In a large bowl, whisk together flour, brown sugar, baking powder, baking soda, cinnamon, nutmeg, and salt.

Combine Wet Ingredients:
- In another bowl, whisk together buttermilk, egg, melted butter, vanilla extract, and mashed sweet potatoes.

Combine Mixtures:

- Pour the wet ingredients into the dry ingredients and stir until just combined. Do not overmix; a few lumps are okay.

Preheat Griddle or Pan:

- Preheat a griddle or non-stick pan over medium heat.

Cook Pancakes:

- Pour 1/4 cup portions of batter onto the griddle for each pancake. Cook until bubbles form on the surface, then flip and cook until the other side is golden brown.

Serve:

- Serve the Sweet Potato Pancakes warm.

Optional Toppings:

- Drizzle with maple syrup and sprinkle with chopped nuts if desired.

Enjoy these flavorful and slightly sweet Sweet Potato Pancakes for a delightful breakfast or brunch!

Breakfast Flatbread

Ingredients:

- 2 whole wheat flatbreads or naan
- 4 large eggs
- 1 cup cherry tomatoes, halved
- 1/2 cup feta cheese, crumbled
- 1/4 cup red onion, thinly sliced
- Fresh spinach leaves
- Olive oil
- Salt and black pepper to taste
- Fresh herbs (e.g., parsley or chives) for garnish (optional)

Instructions:

Preheat Oven:
- Preheat your oven to 375°F (190°C).

Prepare Flatbreads:
- Place the flatbreads on a baking sheet. Lightly brush them with olive oil.

Add Toppings:
- Scatter cherry tomatoes, crumbled feta cheese, and thinly sliced red onion over the flatbreads.

Create Wells for Eggs:
- Use the back of a spoon to create small wells in the toppings to hold the eggs.

Crack Eggs:
- Crack one egg into each well on the flatbreads.

Season:

- Sprinkle salt and black pepper over the eggs and toppings.

Bake:

- Bake in the preheated oven for 12-15 minutes or until the egg whites are set but the yolks are still slightly runny.

Add Fresh Spinach:

- In the last few minutes of baking, scatter fresh spinach leaves over the flatbreads to wilt slightly.

Garnish:

- Garnish with fresh herbs if desired.

Serve:

- Serve the Breakfast Flatbreads warm.

Enjoy these Breakfast Flatbreads with a combination of eggs, tomatoes, feta, and spinach for a satisfying and flavorful breakfast or brunch!

Breakfast Enchiladas

Ingredients:

For the Filling:

- 8 large eggs
- 1/4 cup milk
- Salt and black pepper to taste
- 1 tablespoon olive oil
- 1/2 cup diced onion
- 1/2 cup diced bell peppers (any color)
- 1 cup cooked and diced breakfast sausage or bacon
- 1 cup shredded cheddar or Mexican blend cheese

For the Enchilada Sauce:

- 2 tablespoons unsalted butter
- 2 tablespoons all-purpose flour
- 1 1/2 cups chicken or vegetable broth
- 1/2 cup tomato sauce
- 1 teaspoon ground cumin
- 1 teaspoon chili powder
- Salt to taste

For Assembly:

- 8 small flour tortillas
- 1 cup shredded cheese for topping

- Fresh cilantro, chopped (for garnish)
- Sour cream and salsa (for serving, optional)

Instructions:

For the Filling:

Prepare Eggs:
- In a bowl, whisk together eggs, milk, salt, and black pepper.

Cook Eggs:
- In a skillet, heat olive oil over medium heat. Add diced onion and bell peppers, sauté until softened. Pour the egg mixture into the skillet and scramble until cooked through. Add cooked and diced breakfast sausage or bacon. Remove from heat and stir in shredded cheese until melted.

For the Enchilada Sauce:

Make Roux:
- In a saucepan, melt butter over medium heat. Stir in flour to create a roux.

Add Broth and Spices:
- Gradually whisk in chicken or vegetable broth. Add tomato sauce, ground cumin, chili powder, and salt. Continue to whisk until the sauce thickens. Remove from heat.

Assembly:

Preheat Oven:
- Preheat your oven to 375°F (190°C).

Fill Tortillas:

- Place a portion of the egg and sausage mixture onto each flour tortilla. Roll them up and place them seam-side down in a baking dish.

Pour Sauce:

- Pour the enchilada sauce over the rolled tortillas.

Top with Cheese:

- Sprinkle shredded cheese over the top.

Bake:

- Bake in the preheated oven for 20-25 minutes or until the enchiladas are heated through and the cheese is melted and bubbly.

Garnish:

- Garnish with chopped cilantro.

Serve:

- Serve the Breakfast Enchiladas warm with sour cream and salsa if desired.

These Breakfast Enchiladas are a flavorful and satisfying option for a hearty breakfast or brunch!

www.ingramcontent.com/pod-product-compliance
Lightning Source LLC
LaVergne TN
LVHW081550060526
838201LV00054B/1838